SURVIVAL
ARABIC

How to Communicate Without Fuss or Fear—Instantly!

by Fethi Mansouri
&
Yousef Alreemawi

TUTTLE PUBLISHING
Tokyo • Rutland, Vermont • Singapore

Published by Periplus Editions (HK) Ltd. with editorial offices at 364 Innovation
Drive, North Clarendon, Vermont 05759 U.S.A. and 61 Tai Seng Avenue
#02-12, Singapore 534167

LCC Card No. 2004300390
ISBN-13: 978-0-8048-3861-0
ISBN-10: 0-8048-3861-5

Distributed by:

Asia Pacific
Berkeley Books Pte. Ltd.
61 Tai Seng Avenue #02-12,
Singapore 534167
Tel: (65) 6280-1330; Fax: (65) 6280-6290
inquiries@periplus.com.sg
www.periplus.com

North America, Latin America & Europe
Tuttle Publishing, 364 Innovation Drive
North Clarendon, VT 05759-9436 U.S.A.
Tel: 1 (802) 773-8930; Fax: 1 (802) 773-6993
info@tuttlepublishing.com
www.tuttlepublishing.com

Japan
Tuttle Publishing, Yaekari Building, 3F
5-4-12 Osaki, Shinagawa-ku,
Tokyo 141-0032, Japan
Tel: (81) 3 5437-0171; Fax: (81) 3 5437-0755
tuttle-sales@gol.com

11 10 09 08 07   6 5 4 3 2 1

Printed in Singapore

Contents

Introduction

How frustrating it can be when communicating with people is difficult! Millions of people who visit the Arab world every year go from being literate in their homelands to not being able to speak, read or understand a word in Arabic. The use of English in Arabic-speaking countries is still very limited. Aside from the traveler's frustration, where visiting businesspeople are concerned, the hurdle of not being able to communicate even at a very basic level can have serious consequences.

Most people use fewer than 1,000 words of their first language to handle their daily activities. What those words are and the way they are employed are more important than their number, especially when it comes to using a second language. With a vocabulary of a few hundred Arabic words, you can communicate a lot of ideas not only to "survive" occasions you might find yourself in during your visit(s) to an Arabic-speaking country, but also to enjoy yourself a bit more.

Survival Arabic's approach is all about providing you with words, expressions and phrases commonly used in Arab societies, and supplying them both in helpful romanized transliteration and in Arabic characters. We hope this book helps you take the first step to communicating in Arabic with those who speak it.

How to Use This Book

There are at least ten Arabic dialects used throughout the Arabic world, and although they belong to the same family, they may be as different as French, Italian, Spanish and other Latin-Romance languages are from one another. Modern Standard Arabic (MSA) is the bridge for all these Arabic dialects; it is a tool by which all Arabs can communicate with one another. *Survival Arabic* is based on MSA with very few references to colloquial Arabic.

In addition to the Arabic characters, a transliteration using the more familiar English alphabet is provided to help you pronounce the word, phrase or sentence correctly. At the beginning of this book is an invaluable pronunciation guide which is based on imitation sounds—whereby you can learn to read Arabic using as an aid the English that you're familiar with.

Notes on Pronunciation

Arabic Letter	English Transliteration	Approximate sound in English
أ	a	*a* (as in **a**t)
ب	b	*b*
ت	t	*t*
ث	<u>th</u>	*th* (as in **th**ree)
ج	j	*j* (as in **j**elly)
ح	<u>h</u>	No English equivalent. An emphatic *h* sound, from the back of the throat.
خ	<u>kh</u>	Similar to the *ch* in the Scottish word lo**ch** or the German name Ba**ch**.
د	d	*d*
ذ	<u>dh</u>	*th* (as in **th**ere)
ر	r	a rolled *r* sound
ز	z	*z*
س	s	*s*
ش	<u>sh</u>	*sh* (as in **sh**ine)
ص	<u>s</u>	Like *s*, but very heavily pronounced.
ض	<u>d</u>	Like *d*, but very heavily pronounced.

ط	t̲	Like *t*, but very heavily pronounced.
ظ	z̲	Like *z*, but very heavily pronounced.
ع	ʿ	No English equivalent. The 'ayn: A constriction of the throat. You can produce it by saying an *aargh* sound, from the throat as if swallowing the sound.
غ	g̲h̲	No English equivalent. An *r* in the back of the throat (similar to French *r*).
ف	f	*f*
ق	q	A *k* sound from deep in the back of the throat.
ك	k	*k*
ل	l	*l*
م	m	*m*
ن	n	*n*
ه	h	*h*
و	w	*w* (as in **w**as)
ي	y	*y* (as in **y**ellow)

Vowels

In standard Arabic, there are three short and three long vowels.

Short Vowels

Short vowels are small signs written above or under the consonants after which they are to be pronounced. A text in which vowels are marked is called "vocalized" text. But in modern written texts most short vowels are not indicated at all. This means that a knowledge of Arabic vocabulary and grammar is necessary to read "unvocalized" written text (where vowels are not indicated).

Vowel	Sign		Sound in English
a	´	(fathah)	as in "had"
i	ˌ	(kasrah)	as in "it"
u	´	(dammah)	as in "put"

Arabic short vowels and diacritics are optional elements that are used occasionally to disambiguate homographs when there is insufficient context for the reader to do so. In Survival Arabic, short vowels and diacritics are written when potential ambiguities are anticipated, such as to disambiguate the Arabic for "Amman" and "Oman" or to indicate the passive voice as in the following example:

to write kataba   كَتَبَ

is written kutiba   كُتِبَ

The verb will mostly appear without short vowels as كتب, and the context will tell us if the verb was active or passive. Short vowels and diacritics are useful for learners, but once you know the language they are more of a hindrance. Apart from religious and poetry texts, Arabs rarely use short vowels and diacritics.

Long Vowels

The three long vowels are

Vowel	Sign	Sound in English
aa	ا	as in "far" but longer
ii	ي	as in "see"
uu	و	as in "noon"

Doubling of a consonant

The mark ˝ is called **shaddah** and it denotes doubling a consonant, which involves pronouncing it twice, such as the double *k* in "book**k**eeping" and the double *n* in "non-**n**ative." A **shaddah** is placed on the doubled consonant and must carry one of the three short vowels indicated above.

The maddah

A wavy line (~) called a **maddah** is written above the long vowel (ا) aa as in آ to indicate a glottal stop or catch, followed by a long vowel. A glottal stop sounds like a break in the voice. The sudden stop in the English "uh-oh" is an example of the glottal stop principle.

mirror   **mir'aah**   مرآة

Koran   **qur'aan**   قرآن

Notes on Grammar

1. Personal Pronouns

anaa	أنـا	I
anti	أنـت	you (sing., fem.)
huwa	هـو	he
hiya	هـي	she
anta	أنـت	you (sing., masc.)
humaa	هـمـا	they (dual*)
antumaa	أنـتـمـا	you (dual*)
nahnu	نـحـن	we
antum	أنـتـم	you (pl., masc.)
antunna	أنـتـمـا	you (pl., fem.)
hum	هـم	they (pl., masc.)
hunna	هـنَّ	they (pl., fem.)

*Used when referring to two of anything.

2. Possessive adjectives

A possessive adjective agrees in gender and in number with the noun it refers to (the owner). The following table using the example `**kitaab** ("book") to illustrate the way possessives are marked in Arabic:

kitaab**ii**	ـي	my book
kitaab**uka**	ـكَ	your (masc.) book

kitaabu**ki**	كِ	your (fem.) book
kitaabu**hu**	هُ	his book
kitaabu**ha**	ها	her book
kitaabu**humaa**	هما	their (dual) book
kitaabu**kumaa**	كما	your (dual) book
kitaabu**naa**	نا	our book
kitaabu**kum**	كم	your (pl., masc.) book
kitaabu**kunna**	كن	your (pl., fem.) book
kitaabu**hum**	هم	their (pl., masc.) book
kitaabu**hunna**	هن	their (pl., fem.) book

3. Gender in Nouns

In Arabic, nouns are either masculine or feminine. There are two types of nouns. With regular nouns, the feminine form can be derived from the masculine form by adding a feminine marker suffix (**-at**). For example:

English meaning	Masculine	Feminine
student	taalib طالب	taalib**at** طـالبة
teacher	mudarris مـدرس	mudarris**at** مدرسة

The other class of nouns is the irregular noun where the masculine and feminine forms do not share the same root and can not be derived from one another. For example:

English meaning	Masculine	Feminine
boy	**walad** ولد	
girl		**bint** بنت
man	**rajul** رجل	
woman		**imra'ah** امرأة

Note that even non-animated objects are obligatorily marked for gender as in the following examples:

house	bayyt (masc.)	بيـت
city	madiinat (fem.)	مديـنـة
country	balad (masc.)	بلـد
pen	qalam (masc.)	قـلـم
table	taawilat (fem.)	طـاولـة

The main clue to gender here is whether the noun has **-at** (ة) at the end or not.

4. Definite articles

Definiteness in Arabic is marked in general by means of the article/**al-**/الـ attached at the beginning of the noun as in the following example:

walad ولد a boy ➔ **al-walad** الـولـد the boy

5. Number in Nouns

Arabic differentiates between singular, dual and plural numbers although the dual form is not used frequently. The dual and the regular plural can be derived from the singular form in the following manner:

	Singular	Dual	Plural
player	laa`ib**at** لاعبة	laa`iba**taan** لاعبتان	laa`ib**aat** لاعبات
teacher	mudarris**at** مدرّسة	mudarrisa**taan** مدرّستان	mudarris**aat** مدرّسات
spectator	mutafarrij**at** متفرّجة	mutafarrija**taan** متفرّجتان	mutafarrij**aat** متفرّجات

The above examples refer to the masculine gender only. Derived nouns take the feminine suffix (**-at**) in the singular form and replace the plural masculine marker (**-uun**) with the plural feminine marker (**-aat**). For example, **mudarrisat** مدرسة meaning "a female teacher" becomes **mudarris-aat** مدرسات meaning "female teachers". The feminine dual form is similar to the masculine with the exception of the feminine marker /**at**/ being inserted before the dual form: mudarris-**at-aan** "two female teachers".

6. Verbs

There are two different types of verbs in Arabic depending on their tense/mood: perfective (action complete), and imperfective (action incomplete). Verbs are marked for person, number and gender.

7. Person

In Arabic first, second and third persons are marked differently onto the verb form. Consider the following examples:

I study.	anaa `adrusu	أنـا أدرس
He studies.	huwa **ya**drusu	هـو يدرس
He studied.	huwa darasa	هـو درس
You (sing., masc.) study.	anta **ta**drusu	أنـت تدرس
You (sing., masc.) studied.	anta daras**ta**	أنـت درسـت

8. Gender in Verbs

Verbs inherently exhibit gender marking in both perfective (past) and imperfective (present) forms. The gender marking paradigm for perfective verbs is as follows:

The boy ate.	al-waladu akal**a**	الـولـد أكـل
The girl ate.	al-bintu akal**at**	الـبـنـت أكـلـت

So the /**t**/ sound in the second example marks a feminine gender at the verb ending (suffix). Gender in imperfective verbs is marked by means of prefixes using the /**y**/ and /**t**/ sounds to signal feminine and masculine respectively:

The boy eats /is eating.	al-waladu **ya**`kulu	الـولـد يـأكـل
The girl eats /is eating	al-bintu **ta**`kulu	الـبـنـت تـأكـل

9. Negation

Negation is expressed differently for nominal as opposed to verbal sentences. When negating nominal and adjectival phrases, "**laysa**" and its variations are used as in the examples below.

10. The nominal negation word "laysa" ليــس

This is always inserted before or after the pronoun/noun to which it refers as shown in the following example:

I am not angry. **lastu ghaadiban** لـــست غـاضـبـا

Here are the various forms of "laysa" with the main pronouns:

you (sing., masc.)	anta	lasta	لــست َ
you (sing., fem.)	anti	lasti	لــست ِ
he	huwa	laysa	لـيـس
she	hiya	laysat	لـيـست
I	anaa	lastu	لــست ُ
we	nahnu	lasnaa	لــسـنـا
they (masc.)	hum	laysuu	لـيـسـوا
you (pl., masc.)	antum	lastum	لــسـتـم
you (pl., fem.)	antunna	lastunna	لــسـتـن ّ

11. Verbal negation words

There are four verbal negation words used to negate verbs/ actions in the present, past and the future respectively. These are shown in the following examples:

Negation Word		Tense	Example		Meaning
laa	لا	Present	**laa** ashrab	لا أشـرب	I don't drink.
lan	لــن	Future	**lan** ashrab	لــن أشـــرب	I won't drink.
lam	لـم	Past	**lam** ashrab	لــم أشـــرب	I did not drink.
maa	لـا	Past/ Continuing	**maa** sharibtu	مـا شـربـت	I have not drunk.

Greetings

Peace be upon you.
The most common Arabic greeting is
as-salaamu `alaykum السلام عليكم, an Islamic greet-
ing that is used by Muslims and non-Muslims alike.

And upon you be peace.
The response to the previous greeting:
wa `alayykumus salaam وعليكم السلام

Hello. marhaban مرحبا

Welcome. ahlan wa sahlan أهلا وسهلا

Welcome to you. ahlan bikum أهلا بكم

Good morning. sabaahal khayr صباح الخير

Good evening. masaa`al khayr مساء الخير

Not too bad. laa ba`s لا بأس

It has been so long, hasn't it?
laqad marra waqtun tawiil, alaysa kadhaalik?
لقد مر وقت طويل، أليس كذلك؟

I have been so busy.
kuntu mashghuulan jiddan كنت مشغولا جدًا

I have been away. kuntu musaafiran كنت مسافراً

How are you? kayfal ḥaal? كيف الحال؟

I am fine, thanks.
anaa bikhayr shukran أنا بخير شكراً

I am not very well.
lastu `alaa maa yuraam لست على ما يرام

Have a good night. tusbiḥ `alaa khayr تصبح على خير

See you tomorrow. araaka ghadan أراك غداً

See you next week.
araakal `usbuu`al qaadim أراك الأسبوع القادم

Take care! diir baalak `ala ḥaalak دير بالك على حالك

Greeting Etiquette

As in most cultures, men shake hands. Also, it is a sign of friendship if friends keep holding each other's hands for a while after the initial handshake. Close friends may kiss on the cheeks (at least twice), and this is particularly the case among women.

Some Muslims, especially in the Gulf countries, hold the belief that unnecessary eye or physical contact between unrelated men and women should be avoided. Therefore, it is not recommended, if you are a man, to extend your hand to women for a handshake. Similarly, you may find, if you are a woman, that some men will refrain from stretching out their hands to you. This does not mean that they don't respect or welcome you; it is just a reflection of the conservative society in which opposite sexes can't mix the way they do in the West.

This also means that some people will be offended if a stranger tries to shake hands with (or hug or kiss!) their female relatives. In the same way, it is against the custom to pat members of the opposite sex on their shoulders, arms or backs, or seek any physical contact with them.

Arabic Names

Unlike English first names, the meanings of most Arabic first names are still clearly linked to social values and customs. Parents often choose the names of their newborn babies because of the meanings attached. Here are some examples of the more common names:

MEN'S NAMES

Jamaal	جمـــال	**beauty**
Naadir	نـــادر	**rare**
Sayyf	سـيـف	**sword**
Kariim	كـريـم	**generous**
Saabir	صـــابـر	**patient**

Shariif شَرِيف	honorable
Muhammad مُحَمَّد	highly praised
Usaamah أُسَامَة	lion

WOMEN'S NAMES

Amal أَمَل	hope
Najaah نَجَاح	success
Hanaan حَنَان	tenderness
Amiinah أَمِينَة	trustworthy
Ibtisaam ابْتِسَام	smile
Nafiisah نَفِيسَة	valuable
Sakiinah سَكِينَة	tranquility
Rubaa رُبَى	hills

Some names have biblical origins:

Jesus	Iisaa عِيسَى
Mary	Maryam مَرْيَم
Moses	Muusaa مُوسَى
Abraham	Ibraahiim ابْرَاهِيم
Joseph	Yuusuf يُوسُف
Ismael	Ismaa`iil اسْمَاعِيل
David	Daawuud دَاوُود
Solomon	Sulayymaan سُلَيْمَان

There are names that bear a strong religious character. In Islam, God—Allah—has ninety-nine names. It is very common to form a masculine name by combining the word `**abd** عَبْد (meaning "he who worships" or "the slave of") with one of Allah's names.

"he who worships God" `abdullaah   عـبـد الله

"he who worships the Creator"
`abdul-<u>kh</u>aaliq   عـبـد الخـالـق

"he who worships the Peace"
`abdus-salaam   عـبـد الـسـلام

"he who worships the Merciful"
`abdur-ra<u>h</u>maan   عبـد الرحمن

"he who worships the Glorious"
`abdul-majiid   عـبـد المجيد

Surnames or family names are a relatively new phenomenon in Arab countries. Traditionally, a person would be identified as "the son of his father". This is done by using the word "son" **ibn** ابـن or **bin** بـن:
Mu<u>h</u>ammad, son of Abdullah
mu<u>h</u>ammad ibn `abdullaah   مـحـمـد بـن عـبـد الله

The word **bint** بـنـت "daughter" goes with women's names:
Laila, daughter of Ali laylaa bint `alii   لـيـلـى بـنـت عـلي

The words **ibn** and **bint** are not used often these days. Instead, the father's first name follows his child's name, e.g. Yousef's son would be
Firas the son of Ahmad Yousef فـراس أحمـد يـوسف
Maryam, the daughter of Abdel-Icareem Al-Hussar

Maryam Abdul-Kareem Al-Hussari

مريم عبد الكريم الحصري

Upon marriage, a woman doesn't take her husband's name and keeps her name as it is.

After having a child of their own, the couple will be known, informally, as the parents of the eldest son or, in the absence of a son, daughter. So if Ali was born to Muhammad and Ḥanaan, Muhammad will become known as Ali's father, **abu `alii** علي أبو;
and Hanaan will become known as Ali's mother,
`umm `alii أم علي.

Family Terms

family	`aa'ilah	عائلة
father	`ab	أب
mother	`umm	أَم
husband	zawj	زوج
wife	zawjah	زوجة
son	ibn	ابن
daughter	ibnah	ابنة
boy	walad	ولد
girl	bint	بنت
brother	`akh	أخ
sister	`ukht	أخت
grandfather	jadd	جَد

grandmother	jaddah	جدّة
uncle (paternal)	`amm	عمّ
uncle (maternal)	khaal	خـال
aunt (paternal)	`ammah	عمّة
aunt (maternal)	khaalah	خـالـة
grandson	hafiid	حـفـيـد
granddaughter	hafiidah	حـفـيـدة
father-in-law	hamaa	حما
mother-in-law	hamaah	حمـاة
niece (brother's dau.)	bint `akh	بنـت أخ
niece (sister's dau.)	bint `ukht	بنت أخت
nephew (brother's son)	ibn `akh	ابن أخ
nephew (sister's son)	ibn `ukht	ابن أخت

Do you have children?
hal `indaka abnaa`? هـل عـنـدك أبـنـاء ؟

I have two sons. `indii waladaan عـنـدي ولـدان

Are you married?
hal `anta mutazawwij? هـل أنـت مُـتـزوّج ؟

I am not married.
anaa lastu mutazawwijan أنـا لـسـت مـتـزوجـاً

I am single. `anaa a`zab أنـا أعـزب

This is my husband. haadhaa zawjii هـذا زوجـي

This is my wife. haadhihi zawjatii هـذه زوجـتـي

Getting Introduced

name	ism	اسـم
I.D. card	biṭaaqat hawiyyah	بطـاقـة هـويـة
title	laqab	لقـب

Allow me to introduce myself to you.
ismaḥ lii `an `uqaddima nafsii lak
اسـمـح لـي أن أقـدم نـفـسـي لـك

My name is Mark. ismii maark   اسـمـي مـارك

What's your name? (formal way, roughly translated as
"What's the good name?")
alism alkariim?   الاسـم الكـريـم؟

Would you please introduce yourself to us?
qaddim nafsaka lanaa law samaḥt?
قـدم نـفـسـك لـنـا لـو سـمـحت

Nice to meet you. furṣah sa`iidah   فـرصـة سـعـيـدة

My pleasure. `anaa `as`ad   أنـا أسـعـد

This is Mr. Colin.
haadha huwas sayyid kulin   هـذا هـو الـسـيـد كـولـن

Welcome. ahlan wa sahlan   أهـلاً وسـهـلاً

Please come in. tafaddal biddukhuul تـفـضـل بـالدخول

Please take a seat. tafaddal bil juluus تـفـضـل بـالجـلـوس

Thanks a lot. shukran jaziilan شـكـرا جـزيـلا

Don't mention it/you're welcome.
laa shukra `alla waajib لا شكـر عـلى واجـب

In a Taxi

taxi	sayyaarat `ujrah	سـيـارة أجـرة
stop/stand (n.)	mawqif	مـوقـف
fare	`ujrah	أجـرة
gauge/meter	`addaad	عـدّاد
driver	saa`iq	سـائـق
left (direction)	yasaar	يـسـار
right (direction)	yamiin	يـمـيـن
straight	`alaa tuul	عـلى طـول (colloquial Arabic)
intersection	taqaatu`	تـقـاطـع
corner	rukn	ركـن
address	`unwaan	عـنـوان

I want to go to the airport, please.
uriidu an adh-haba ilaa al-mataar law samaht
أريـد أن أذهـب إلـى الـمـطـار لـو سـمـحـت

I am in a hurry. anaa musta'jil أنا مُستعجِل

How long does it take to reach... ?
kam minal waqt nahtaaj linasila 'ilaa ... ?
كم من الوقت نحتاج لنصل إلى.....؟

Please come and pick me up at 9:00 a.m.
arjuu an ta'tiya lita'khudhanii fis saa'atit taasi'ati sabaahan
أرجو أن تأتي لتأخذني في الساعة
التاسعة صباحاً

Take me to this address, please.
khudhnii 'ilaa haadhal 'unwaan law samaht
خذني إلى هذا العنوان لو سمحت

Could you please wait for me?
intazirnii min fadlik? انتظرني من فضلك؟

How much is the fare, please?
kam al'ujrah law samaht? كم الأجرة لو سمحت؟

Please go straight ahead.
'ala tuul law samaht على طول لو سمحت

Please turn right here.
'ilaa yamiin law samaht إلى اليمن لو سمحت

please turn left at the next street.
'alal yasaar minash shaari' attaalii على اليسار من الشارع التالي

I will be back in 5 minutes.
sa'a'uudu ba'da <u>kh</u>amsi daqaa'iq

سـأعـود بـعـد خـمـس دقـائـق

At the Hotel

hotel	funduq	فـنـدق
reservations	al-<u>h</u>ujuuza*at*	الـحـجـوزات
room	<u>gh</u>urfah	غـرفـة
suite	janaa<u>h</u>	جنـاح
swimming pool	masba<u>h</u>	مـسـبـح
reception	'istiqbaal	استـقـبـال
receptionist	muwa<u>zz</u>af istiqbaal	موظـف استـقـبـال
lobby	rudhah	ردهـة
elevator	ma<u>s</u>'ad kahrabaa'iyy	مصعد كـهـربـائي
stairs	daraj	درج
vacation	ijaazah	إجازة
single	mufrad	مـفـرد
double	muzdawaj	مـزدوج
bed	sariir	سرير
large	kabiir	كبير
small	<u>sagh</u>iir	صغير
clean	na<u>z</u>iif	نظيف
cleaner/maid	'aamil anna<u>z</u>aafah	عامل النظافة
room number	raqm al<u>gh</u>urfah	رقم الغرفة
key	miftaa<u>h</u>	مفتاح
air conditioning	takyiif hawaa'	تكييف هواء

blanket	g̲h̲iṭaa` غطاء
pillow	wisaadah وسادة
laundry	g̲h̲asiil غسيـل
luggage	amti`ah أمـتـعـة
tip	baqs̲h̲iis̲h̲ بقشيش (colloquial Arabic)
emergency exit	mak̲h̲raj aṭṭawaari` مخرج الطوارئ
bathroom	ḥammaam حمَام

My name is Yousef; I have a reservation.

ismii yuusif, `indii ḥajz اسمي يوسف، عندي حجز

Do you have a vacant room?

hal `indaka g̲h̲urfah s̲h̲aag̲h̲irah?

هـل عـنـدك غـرفـة شـاغـرة؟

What's my room number?

maa raqmu g̲h̲urfatii? مـا رقـم غـرفـتـي؟

Do you have a single room?

hal `indaka g̲h̲urfah bisariir mufrad?

هـل عـنـدك غـرفـة بسـريـر مـفـرد؟

Do you have a double room?

hal `indaka g̲h̲urfah bisariir muzda waj?

هـل عـنـدك غـرفـة بسـريـر مزدوج؟

The room is too small.

alg̲h̲urfah s̲aghiirah jiddan الغرفة صغيرة جدًّا

Do you have a larger room?

hal `indaka ghurfah akbar? هـل عـنـدك غـرفـة أكبر؟

I want a room for two nights.

`uriidu ghurfah lilaylatayn أريـد غـرفـة لـلـيـلـتـين

I want a room with a sea view.

`uriidu ghurfatan tuṭillu `alal baḥr
أريـد غـرفـة تـطـلّ عـلى الـبـحـر

What is the rate for this room?

kam ujratu haadhihil ghurfah? كـم أجـرة هـذه الـغـرفـة؟

What time does the restaurant open?

mataa yaftaḥul maṭ`am? مـتـى يفتح الـمـطـعـم؟

Please send someone to clean my room.

`arsil man yunaẓẓifal ghurfah min faḍlik
أرسـل مـن يـنـظف الـغـرفة مـن فـضـلـك

What time is breakfast? matal `ifṭaar? مـتـى الإفـطـار؟

Please wake me up at 7 a.m.

`arjuu an tuuqiẓanii fis saa`atis saabi`ah
أرجـو أن تـوقـظـنـي فـي الـسـاعـة الـسـابـعـة

Is there an English newspaper?

hal yuujadu jariidah bil-inkliiziyyah?
هـل هـنـاك جـريـدة بـالإنـجـلـيـزيّـة؟

Where can I get a map?

min ayna yumkin an ahsula `alaa khariitah?

من أين يمكن أن أحصل على خريطة؟

I have lost my room key.

laqad ada`tu miftaaha ghurfatii

لقد أضعت مفتاح غرفتي

Are there any messages for me?

hal hunaaka ayyatu rasaa'il lii?   هل هناك أية رسائل لي؟

I have some laundry.

`indii ba`dul ghasiil   عندي بعض الغسيل

I need another blanket.

`ahtaaju `ilaa ghitaa'in aakhar   أحتاج إلى غطاء آخر

When will the laundry be ready?

mataa sayakuunul ghasiil jaahiz?

متى سيكون الغسيل جاهزاً؟

I would like to extend my reservation.

`awaddu an `umaddida hajzii   أود أن أمدد حجزي

I would like to stay for two more days.

`awaddu an abqaa li yawmayyn `idaafiyyayn

أود أن أبقى ليومين إضافيين

How far is it from the hotel?
kam huwa ba`iid minal funduq?
كـم هـو بـعـيـد مـن الـفـنـدق؟

Can I walk there from the hotel?
hal yumkinunii an 'amshii `ilaa hunaak minal funduq?
هـل يـمـكـنـني أن أمـشـي إلـى هـنـاك مـن الـفـنـدق؟

Please call a taxi for me.
utlub sayyarata `ujrah minfadlik
اطلب سـيـارة أجـرة مـن فـضـلـك

What time is checkout?
mataa yajibu an `ughaadir?   مـتى يـجـب أن أغـادر ؟

Asking Questions

(for Yes/No questions)	hal	هـل
who?	man?	مَـن؟
what?	maadhaa/maa?	مـاذا / مـا؟
when?	mataa?	مـتى
where?	ayna?	أيـن؟
how much/many?	kam?	كـم؟
how?	kayfa?	كـيـف؟
why?	limaadhaa?	لـمـاذا؟

nationality	jinsiyyah جنسية
American	amriikiyy أمريكيّ
Australian	'usturaaliyy أستراليّ
British	briitaaniyy بريطانيّ
Canadian	kanadiyy كنديّ
Chinese	ṣiiniyy صينيّ
Dutch	hulandiyy هولنديّ
French	faransiyy فرنسيّ
German	almaaniyy ألمانيّ
country	dawlah دولة
America	amriikaa أمريكا
Australia	'usturaalyaa أستراليا
Britain	briitaanyaa بريطانيا
Canada	kanadaa كندا
China	aṣ-ṣiin الصين
France	faransaa فرنسا
Germany	almaanyaa ألمانيا
New Zealand	nyuuziilandah نيوزيلندة
continent	qaarrah قارّة
city	madiinah مدينة
province	muḥaafaẓah محافظة
state	wilaayah ولاية

YES/NO

Are you Italian? hal anta `iiṭaaliyy? هـل أنـت إيـطـالـي؟

No, I am Australian.
laa, anaa 'usturaaliyy لا، أنـا أسـتـرالـي

Are you German? hal anta almaaniyy? هـل أنـت ألـمـانـي؟

Yes, I am. na`am, anaa almaanee نـعـم أنـا ألـمـانـي

WHO

Who are you? man anta? مَـن أنـت؟

Who is that man? man dhaalikar rajul? مَـن ذلـك الـرجُـل؟

Who speaks English here?
man yataḥaddathu al-inghliiziyyah hunaa?
مـن يتـحـدّث الإنجلـيـزيـة هـنا؟

Whose car is this?
sayyaaratu man haa dhih? سـيـارة مـن هـذه؟

Whose bags are those?
ḥaqaa'ibu man tilk? حـقـائـب مـن تـلـك؟

Whom are you talking to? ma`a man tatakallam?
مـع مـن تـتـكـلـم؟

WHAT

What are you saying? maadhaa taquul? ماذا تقول؟

What is this? maa hadhaa? ما هذا؟

What is this in Arabic?
maa ma`naa dhaalik bil-arabiyyah?
ما معنى ذلك بالعربية؟

What is your address? maa `unwaanuk? ما عنوانك؟

What is the name of this place?
masmu haadhal makaan? ما اسمُ هذا المَكان؟

What's wrong? mal mushkilah? ما المشكلة؟

What would you like to eat?
maadhaa turiidu an ta'kul? ماذا تريد أن تأكل؟

What would you like to drink?
maadhaa turiidu an tashrab? ماذا تريد أن تشرب؟

WHEN

When will we go? mataa sanadhhab? متى سنذهب؟

What time is breakfast? matal 'iftaar? متى الإفطار؟

When does the market open?

mataa yaftahus suuq? مـتـى يـفـتـح الـسـوق؟

When do you have to go?

mataa yajibu an tadh-hab? مـتـى يـجـب أن تـذهب؟

WHERE

Where is the restaurant? 'aynal mat`am? أيـن المَـطـعَـم؟

Where is the hotel? 'aynal funduq? أيـن الـفُـنـدُق؟

Where are you from? min 'ayna 'anta? مِن أيـن أنـت؟

Where are we going?

'ilaa 'ayna nahnu dhaahibuun? إلى أين نـحنُ ذاهـبـون؟

Where do you want to go?

'ilaa 'ayna turiidu an tadh-hab? إلـى أيـن تـريد أن تـذهب؟

Where is the bus stop? 'ayna mawqiful baas?
أيـن مـوقـف الـبـاص؟

Where is the toilet? 'aynal hammaam? أيـن الـحـمّـام؟

How much does this shirt cost?

bi kam haa<u>dh</u>al qamiis? بكم هذا القميص؟

How long will you stay here?

kam satabqaa hunaa? كم ستبقى هنا؟

How long does the train trip to Cairo take?

kam ta'<u>kh</u>udhu ri<u>h</u>latu bilqi<u>t</u>aar 'ilal qaahirah?
كم تأخذ الرحلة بالقطار إلى القاهرة؟

How are you? kayfa <u>h</u>aaluk? كيف حالك؟

How can I get to the market?

kayfa yumkin an a<u>dh</u>-haba 'ilaa suuq?
كيف يمكن أن أذهب إلى السوق؟

Going Somewhere

cinema	sinamaa	سينما
bar/pub	<u>h</u>aanah	حانة
restaurant	ma<u>t</u>`am	مطعم
theater	masra<u>h</u>	مسرح
bank	bank	بنك
picnic	ri<u>h</u>lah	رحلة
north	<u>sh</u>amaal	شمال

south	januub	جنوب
east	sharq	شرق
west	gharb	غرب
right	yamiin	يمين
left	yasaar	يسار
in front of	'amaam	أمام
behind	khalf	خلف
beside	bi jaanib	بجانب
near	qariib	قريب
far	ba`iid	بعيد
above	fawq	فوق
under	taht	تحت

I want to go and see a movie.
'uriidu an ushaahida film   أريد أن أشاهد فيلم

Oh! That's a good idea! fikrah yajjidah!   فكرة جيدة!

Would you like to go with me?
hal tawaddu an ta'tii ma`ii?   هل تود أن تأتي معي؟

I am afraid I can't this evening.
'akhshaa annanii laa astatii` haadhal masaa'
أخشى أنني لا أستطيع هذا المساء

How about tomorrow? bukra? (colloquial Arabic)   بكرة؟

Yes, that would be good.
na`am, haadhihi fikratun jayyidah   نعم هذه فكرة جيدة

I am sorry. I have an appointment.
'anaa aasif, `indii maw`id آسـف، عـنـدي مـوعـد

Let's go for a walk.
fal natama<u>sh</u>-<u>sh</u>aa qaliilan فـلـنـتـمـشـى قـلـيـلا

Let's go to a falafel restaurant.
fal na<u>dh</u>-hab 'ilaa ma<u>t</u>`am falaafil
فـلـنـذهـب إلـى مـطـعـم فـلافـل

Is it nearby? hal huwa qariib? هـل هـو قـريـب؟

Can we walk there?
mumkin 'an nam<u>sh</u>ii 'ilaa hunaak?
مـمـكـن أن نـمـشـي إلـى هـنـاك؟

No, let's take a taxi.
laa, lina'<u>kh</u>u<u>dh</u> sayyaarata 'ujrah لا لـنـأخـذ سـيـارة أجرة

Cardinal Numbers

0	<u>s</u>ifr	٠
1	waa<u>h</u>id	١
2	i<u>th</u>naan	٢
3	<u>th</u>alaa<u>th</u>ah	٣
4	arba`ah	٤
5	<u>kh</u>amsah	٥

6	sittah	٦
7	sab`ah	٧
8	thamaaniyah	٨
9	tis`ah	٩
10	`asharah	١٠
11	ahada`ashar	١١
12	ithnaa `ashar	١٢
13	thalaathata `ashar	١٣
14	`arba`ata `ashar	١٤
15	khamsata `ashar	١٥
16	sittata `ashar	١٦
17	sab`ata `ashar	١٧
18	thamaaniyata `ashar	١٨
19	tis`ata `ashar	١٩
20	`ishruun	٢٠
21	waahid wa`ishruun	٢١
22	ithnaan wa`ishruun	٢٢
23	thalaathah wa`ishruun	٢٣
24	`arba`ah wa`ishruun	٢٤
25	khamsah wa`ishruun	٢٥
26	sittah wa`ishruun	٢٦
27	sab`ah wa`ishruun	٢٧
28	thamaaniyah wa`ishruun	٢٨
29	tis`ah wa`ishruun	٢٩
30	thalaathuun	٣٠
40	`arba`uun	٤٠
50	khamsuun	٥٠
60	sittuun	٦٠
70	sab`uun	٧٠

80	<u>th</u>amaanuun ٨٠
90	tis'uun ٩٠
100	mi'ah ١٠٠
101	mi'ah wawaa<u>h</u>id ١٠١
102	mi'ah wa'i<u>th</u>naan ١٠٢
103	mi'ah wa<u>th</u>alaa<u>th</u>ah ١٠٣
104	mi'ah wa'arba'ah ١٠٤
105	mi'ah wa<u>kh</u>amsah ١٠٥
106	mi'ah wasittah ١٠٦
107	mi'ah wasab'ah ١٠٧
108	mi'ah wa<u>th</u>amaaniyah ١٠٨
109	mi'ah watis'ah ١٠٩
110	mi'ah wa'a<u>sh</u>arah ١١٠
120	mi'ah wa'i<u>sh</u>ruun ١٢٠
130	mi'ah wa<u>th</u>alaa<u>th</u>uun ١٣٠
140	mi'ah wa'arba'uun ١٤٠
150	mi'ah wa<u>kh</u>amsiin ١٥٠
160	mi'ah wasittuun ١٦٠
170	mi'ah wasab'uun ١٧٠
180	mi'ah wa<u>th</u>amaanuun ١٨٠
190	mi'ah watis'uun ١٩٠
200	mi'ataan ٢٠٠
201	mi'ataan wawaa<u>h</u>id ٢٠١
300	<u>th</u>alaa<u>th</u>umi'ah ٣٠٠
400	arba'u mi'ah ٤٠٠
500	<u>kh</u>amsu mi'ah ٥٠٠
600	sittu mi'ah ٦٠٠
700	sab'u mi'ah ٧٠٠
800	<u>th</u>amaanu mi'ah ٨٠٠

900	tis`u mi'ah ٩٠٠
1,000	`alf ١٠٠٠
1,500	alf wakhamsu mi'ah ١٥٠٠
2,000	alfaan ٢٠٠٠
3,000	thalaathat 'aalaaf ٣٠٠٠
4,000	arba`at 'aalaaf ٤٠٠٠
5,000	khamsat 'aalaaf ٥٠٠٠
6,000	sittat 'aalaaf ٦٠٠٠
7,000	sab`at 'aalaaf ٧٠٠٠
8,000	thamaaniyah 'aalaaf ٨٠٠٠
9,000	tis`at 'aalaaf ٩٠٠٠
10,000	`ashrat 'aalaaf ١٠٠٠٠
11,000	ahada `ashara 'alf ١١٠٠٠
12,000	ithnaa `ashara 'alf ١٢٠٠٠
17,000	sab`ata `ashara 'alf ١٧٠٠٠
100,000	mi'at 'alf ١٠٠٠٠٠
250,000	rub` milyuun ٢٥٠٠٠٠
500,000	nisf milyuun ٥٠٠٠٠٠
1,000,000	milyuun ١٠٠٠٠٠٠

Ordinal Numbers

first	`awwal أوّل
second	thaanii ثانـي
third	thaalith ثالِث
fourth	raabi` رابـع
fifth	khaamis خامـس

sixth	saadis سادِس
seventh	saabi` سابِع
eighth	thaamin ثامِن
ninth	taasi` تاسِع
tenth	`aashir عاشِر
eleventh	haadii `ashar حادي عشر
twelfth	thaanii `ashar ثاني عشر
thirteenth	thaalith `ashar ثالِث عشر
fourteenth	raabi` `ashar رابِع عشر
fifteenth	khaamis `ashar خامِس عشر

Counting People

Numbers 1 and 2: come *after* the noun they modify and
agree with it in gender.

1 (masc.)	waahid واحِد
1 (fem.)	waahidah واحِدة
2 (masc.)	ithnaan اثنان
2 (fem.)	ithnataan اثنتان

I have one brother `indii `akhun waahid عندي أخ واحِد

and two sisters.
wa `ukhtaan ithnataan وأختان اثنتان

Numbers from 3–10: *precede* the noun they describe and
disagree with it in gender; this means that if the noun they
modify is masculine, the numbers are feminine.

3 (masc.)	thalaath	ثلاث
3 (fem.)	thalaathah	ثلاثة
4 (masc.)	'arba`	أربع
4 (fem.)	'arba`ah	أربعة
5 (masc.)	khams	خمس
5 (fem.)	khamsah	خمسة
6 (masc.)	sitt	ست
6 (fem.)	sittah	ستة
7 (masc.)	sab`	سبع
7 (fem.)	sab`ah	سبعة
8 (masc.)	thamaan	ثمان
8 (fem.)	thamaaniyah	ثمانية
9 (masc.)	tis`	تسع
9 (fem.)	tis`ah	تسعة
10 (masc.)	`ashr	عشر
10 (fem.)	`ashrah	عشرة

I have three daughters.

`indii thalaathu banaat عندي ثلاث بنات

I invited four of my (male) friends for dinner.

da`awtu 'arba`atan min asdiqaa'ii `alal `ashaa'
دعوت أربعة من أصدقائي على العشاء

I have three sisters

`indii thalaathu 'akhawaat عندي ثلاث أخوات

and five (male) brothers.

wa arba`atu 'ikhwah وأربعة إخوة

Time Frames

dawn	fajr	فجـر
morning	sabaah	صبـاح
daytime	nahaar	نـهـار
afternoon	`asr	عـصـر
dusk	maghrib	مـغـرب
evening	masaa'	مسـاء
night	layl	ليـل
midnight	muntasaf layl	مـنـتـصـف ليـل
today	al-yawm	اليـوم
tomorrow	ghadan	غدًا
yesterday	`ams	أمـس
day after tomorrow	ba`da ghad	بـعـد غد
every day	kulla yawm	كلّ يـوم
day after day	yawm ba`da yawm	يـوم بـعـد يـوم
in the morning	fis sabaah	في الـصـبـاح
in the afternoon	fiz zuhr	في الظـهـر
this evening	haadhal masaa'	هذا المسـاء
tonight	allaylah	اللـيـلـة
tomorrow morning	ghadan sabaahan	غدًا صبـاحـًا
every morning	kulla sabaah	كل صبـاح
every day	kulla yawm	كل يـوم
every night	kulla layylah	كـل ليـلـة
from now on	minal 'aan fasaa`idan	
		مـن الآن فـصـاعـدًا

Days of the Week

Saturday	assabt	السبت
Sunday	al-`ahad	الأحَد
Monday	al-ithnayn	الإثنين
Tuesday	ath-thulaathaa'	الثلاثاء
Wednesday	al-`arbi`aa'	الأربعاء
Thursday	al-khamiis	الخميس
Friday	al-jum`ah	الجمعة
from Saturday	min assabt	من السبت
until Monday	hattal ithnayyn	حتى الإثنين

What day of the week is today?
ayyu yawmin minal usbuu`i haadhaa?
أي يوم من الأسبوع هذا؟

Today is Monday.
alyawm huwal ith nayn   اليوم هو الإثنين

I am going to Cairo on Wednesday.
sa'adh habu 'ilal qaahirah yawmal arbi`aa'
سأذهب إلى القاهرة يوم الأربعاء

I will return to Damascus on Friday afternoon.
sa'a`uudi 'ilaa dimashq ba`da zuhril khamiis
سأعود إلى دمشق بعد ظهر الخميس

I have a meeting on Thursday.
`indij timaa` yawmal khamiis
عندي اجتماع يوم الخميس

See you next Thursday.

'araakal <u>kh</u>amiis alqaadim   أراك الـخـمـيـس الـقـادم

I am going to see the pyramids this Sunday.

sa'u<u>sh</u>aahidul 'ahraamaat yawmal 'a<u>h</u>ad

سـأشـاهـد الأهـرامـات يـوم الأحـد

Counting Days

one day	yawm waa<u>h</u>id	يـوم واحـد
two days	yawmaan	يـومـان
three days	<u>th</u>alaa<u>th</u>ata 'ayyaam	ثـلاثـة أيّـام
four days	arba`ata 'ayyaam	أربـعـة أيّـام
five days	<u>kh</u>amsata 'ayyaam	خـمسـة أيّـام
six days	sittatata 'ayyaam	ستـة أيّـام
seven days	sab`ata 'ayyaam	سبـعـة أيّـام
eight days	<u>th</u>amaaniyata 'ayyaam	ثـمـانـيـة أيّـام
nine days	tis`ata 'ayyaam	تـسعـة أيّـام
ten days	`a<u>sh</u>rata 'ayyaam	عـشـرة أيّـام
eleven days	ahada `a<u>sh</u>ara yawman	أحد عـشـر يـومـاً
fourteen days	arba`ata `a<u>sh</u>ara yawman	
	أربـعـة عـشـر يـومـاً	
twenty days	`i<u>sh</u>ruun yawman	عـشـرون يـومـاً
thirty days	<u>th</u>alaa<u>th</u>uun yawman	ثلاثون يومـاً
forty days	'arba`uun yawman	أربـعـون يـومـاً
several days	`iddata 'ayyaam	عـدة أيـام
a few days	'ayyaam qaliilah	أيّـام قـلـيـلـة

How many days are we going to stay in Casablanca?

kam yawman sanabqaa fid daaril baydaa'?

كم يـوماً سـنـبـقـى فـي الـدار الـبـيـضـاء؟

I am going to stay there for ten days.

sa'abqaa hunaak li`ashrati ayyaam

سـأبـقـى هـنـاك لـعـشـرة أيّـام

I will take few days off.

sa'u`attil ayyaam qaliilah   ساعطّـل أيّاماً قليلة

How many days will you spend there?

kam yawman satumdii hunaak?

كم يـومـاً سـتـمـضـي هـنـاك؟

I will spend four days.

sa'umdii 'arba`ata 'ayyaam   سـأمـضـي أربـعـة أيّـام

The Weeks

The week in most Arab countries starts on Saturday, the first working day of the week. In these countries, the weekend is on Friday. In Lebanon, for example, where there is a substantial Christian community, Sunday is considered an additional weekend.

this week	haathal 'usbuu` هذا الأسبوع
next week	al-'usbuu` alqaadim الأسبوع القادِم
last week	al-'usbuu` almaadii الأسبوع الماضي
weekend	`utlat nihaayat al'usbuu` عطلة نهاية الأسبوع
from next week	minal 'usbuu`il qaadim من الأسبوع القادم
until next week	hattal 'usbuu`il qaadim حتى الأسبوع القادم

I am going to Amman this week.
'anaa dhaahibun 'ilaa `ammaan haadhal 'usbuu`
أنا ذاهب إلى عمان هذا الأسبوع

I need these documents next week.
'ahtaaju haadhihil wathaa'iq al'usbuu`al qaadim
أحتاج هذه الوثائق الأسبوع القادم

Counting Weeks

one week	'usbuu` waahid أسبوع واحد
two weeks	'usbuu`ayyh أسبوعين
three weeks	thalaathat 'asaabii` ثلاثة أسابيع
four weeks	'arba`at 'asaabii` أربعة أسابيع
five weeks	khamsat 'asaabii` خمسة أسابيع
six weeks	sittatu 'asaabii` ستة أسابيع
seven weeks	sab`atu 'asaabii` سبعة أسابيع

eight weeks	thamaaniyatu 'asaabii'	ثمانية أسابيع
nine weeks	tis'at 'asaabii'	تسعة أسابيع
ten weeks	'asharat 'asaabii'	عشرة أسابيع
twenty weeks	'ishruun 'usbuu'	عشرون أسبوع
fifty-two weeks	ithnaan wa khamsuun 'usbuu'	اثنان وخمسون اسبوع
two weeks ago	qabla 'usbuu'ayn	قبل أسبوعين

three weeks later
ba'da thalaathat 'asaabii'   بعد ثلاثة أسابيع

a few weeks later
ba'da 'asaabii' qaliilah   بعد أسابيع قليلة

I arrived in Dubai two weeks ago.
wasaltu 'iaa dubayy qabla 'usbuu'ayyn
وصلت إلى دبي قبل أسبوعين

I will stay in Tunisia for three more weeks.
sa'abqaa fii tuunis lithalaathati 'asaabii' 'ukhraa
سأبقى في تونس لثلاثة أسابيع أخرى

I am going back in three weeks' time.
sa'a'uudu khilaala sittati 'asaabii'
سأعود خلال ستة أسابيع

I would like to extend my reservation for one more week.
awaddu an 'umaddida hajzii 'usbuu'an
أود أن أمدد حجزي أسبوعاً

The Months

month	<u>sh</u>ahr شــهــر
next month	a<u>sh</u>-<u>sh</u>ahr alqaadim الشــهــر الــقادم
this month	haa<u>dh</u>ash <u>sh</u>ahr هذا الشــهــر
last month	a<u>sh</u>-<u>sh</u>ahr almaa<u>d</u>ii الشهر الماضي
every month	kull <u>sh</u>ahr كــل شــهــر

Calendars in the Arab World
Generally, two calendars are used: the Islamic lunar calendar and the Western solar calendar.

The Islamic Calendar
Some Arab or Islamic countries also use the Hijrii (emigration) calendar in remembrance of Prophet Muhammad's migration from Mecca to Medina.

The first day in this calendar was in the lunar month of Mu<u>h</u>arram, which corresponded with July 16, 622 CE.

This date represents a turning point in the history of Islam's birth and rise and so marks the beginning of the Muslim era or calendar.

The months according to the Hijrii calender are listed below:

1 mu<u>h</u>arram مُحَــرَّم
2 <u>s</u>afar صــفــر
3 rabii` al'awwal ربــيــع الأوّل
4 rabii` a<u>th</u>-<u>th</u>aanii ربــيــع الثــانــي

5 jumaadal ʻuulaa جمـــادى الأولـى
6 jumaadaath thaanii جمــادى الـثاني
7 rajab رجب
8 shaʻbaan شعـبـان
9 ramadaan رمـضـان
10 shawwaal شـوّال
11 dhul qiʻdah ذو الـقـعـدة
12 dhul hijjah ذو الــحـجـة

The month of Ramadaan

Muslims believe that during the month of Ramadaan, Allah revealed the first verses of the Qur'an, the holy book of Islam to the prophet Muhammad, around 610 CE.

Muslims practice sawm صـوم, or fasting, for the entire month of Ramadaan. This means that they abstain from eating and drinking from sunrise till sunset. During Ramadaan and in most Muslim countries most restaurants are closed during the day. Families get up early for suhuur, a meal eaten before the sun rises. After the sun sets, the fast is broken with a meal known as **iftaar** إفـطـار.

The month of shawwaal

Ramadaan ends with a three-day festival of ʻiid al-fitr عـيـد الـفـطـر beginning the first day of **shawwaal**. At ʻiid al-fitr people dress in their best clothes, adorn their homes with lights and decorations, give treats to children, and exchange visits with friends and family.

Pilgrimage

In the twelfth month of the Islamic calendar, **dhul hijjah** ذو الـحـجّـة , Muslims perform **hajj** الـحـج , the pilgrimage to Mecca in Saudi Arabia. The **hajj** is considered one of the five basic requirements of Islam. Its annual observance corresponds with the major holy day `iid al'ad-haa عـيـد الأضـحـى , the second Islamic festival that extends for four days in commemoration of Abraham's readiness to sacrifice his son, Ismael, following divine orders.

While the **hajj** is a religious obligation to be fulfilled at least once in each Muslim's lifetime, religious law allows exemption on grounds of hardship or ill health.

The **hajj** is a series of extensively detailed rituals that include wearing a special garment that symbolizes unity and modesty.

The Western Calendar

It is based on the Gregorian calendar and is called **attaqwiim almiilaadiyy** الـتـقـويـم الـمـيـلادي in reference to the birth of Christ. The abbrevation 'm' م is used to denote it in written schedules, etc.

Today is Tuesday, 19 of Jumaadal 'uulaa 1428 h, 5 of June 2007 AD

alyawm huwa ath-thulaathaa' attaasi` `ashar min jumaadal 'uulaa sanata 'alfin wa 'arba`u mi'ah wa thamaaniyatin wa `ishruun hijrii, alkhaamis min juunyu sanata 'alfayn wa sab`ah miilaadii

اليوم هو الثلاثاء ١٩ جمـادى الأولى ١٤٢٨ هـ ، ٥ ، يونيو ٢٠٠٧ م

The names of the months of the Western calendar vary within Arab countries. In the eastern areas of the region, the names of the indigenous Babylonian-Semitic months are still in use, whereas in Egypt and North African countries, the Gregorian names of the months along with the Babylonian are used.

January	yanaayir	يناير
February	fibraayir	فـبـرايـر
March	maaris	مـارس
April	abriil	أبريل
May	maayu	مـايو
June	yuunyu	يـونـيو
July	yuulyu	يـوليو
August	ughustus	أغسـطـس
September	sibtimbar	سـبـتـمـبر
October	uktubar	أكـتـوبـر
November	nufambar	نـوفـمبـر
December	diisimbar	ديـسـمـبـر

The Babylonian-Semitic months are:

January	a<u>th th</u>aanii	كـانـون الـثـانـي
February	<u>sh</u>ubaa<u>t</u>	شـبـاط
March	aa<u>dh</u>aar	آذار
April	niisaan	نـيـسـان
May	ayyaar	أيـار
June	<u>h</u>uzayyraan	حـزيـران
July	tamuuz	تـمـوز
August	aab	آب
September	ayluul	أيلول

October	tishriin al awwal	تشرين الأول
November	tishriin ath thaanii	تشرين الثاني
December	kanuun al awwal	كانون الأول

I will return this month.

sa'a`uudi haadhash shahr   سأعود هذا الشهر

What's the weather like in July?

kayfal jawwo fii yuulyu?   كيف الجو في يوليو؟

Will the weather get any better next month?

hal sayatahassanul jawwu ash-shahral qaadim?

هل سيتحسن الجو الشهر القادم؟

I will be in Yemen from March till July.

sa'akuunu fil yaman min maaris wa hattaa yulyuu

سأكون في اليمن من مارس وحتى يوليو

It's hot in August in Riyadh.

aljawwu haar fii `ughustus fir riyaad

الجوّ حارّ في أغسطس في الرياض

My birthday is next month.

`iid miilaadii ash-shahral qaadim

عيد ميلادي الشهر القادم

Are you going to be in Beirut in January?

hal satakuunu fii bayruut fii yanaayer?

هل ستكون في بيروت في يناير؟

Counting Months

one month	shahr waahid	شـهـر واحـد
two months	shahrayyn	شـهـرين
three months	thalaathat shuhuur	ثـلاثـة شـهـور
four months	'arba`at shuhuur	أربـعـة شـهـور
five months	khamsat shuhuur	خـمـسـة شـهـور
six months	sittatu shuhuur	ستـة شـهـور
seven months	sab`atu shuhuur	سبـعـة شـهـور
eight months	thamaaniyatu shuhuur	ثمانية شـهـور
nine months	tis`at shuhuur	تـسعـة شـهـور
ten months	'ashrat shuhuur	عـشرة شـهـور
twelve months	ithnaa `ashara shahran	اثنـا عـشـر شـهـراً
a few months	'ash-hur qaliilah	أشـهـر قـلـيـلـة
several months	`iddat shuhuur	عـدة شـهـور

How many months are you going to be here?
kam shahran satabqaa hunaa?   كـم شـهـراً ستـبـقـى هـنـا؟

I will be in Lebanon for two months.
sa'abqaa fii lubnaan li shahrayyn
سـأبـقـى فـي لـبـنـان لـشـهـرين

The project will take several months to finish.
sayastaghriqul mashruu` `iddata ash-hur
سـيـستـغـرق الـمـشـروع عدة أشـهـر

Days of the Month

1st	al'awwal	الأوّل
2nd	althaanii	الثـانـي
3rd	ath thaalith	الثـالِـث
4th	ar raabi`	الرابـع
5th	alkhaamis	الخـامـس
6th	as saadis	السَـادِس
7th	as saabi`	السـابـع
8th	ath thaamin	الثـامِـن
9th	attaasi`	التـاسـع
10th	al`aashir	العـاشِـر
11th	alhaadii `ashar	الحـادي عـشـر
12th	ath thaanii `ashar	الثـانـي عـشـر
13th	ath thaalith `ashar	الثـالِـث عـشـر
14th	ar raabi` `ashar	الرابـع عـشـر
15th	al khaamis `ashar	الخـامـس عـشـر
16th	as saadis `ashar	السادس عـشـر
17th	as saa bi` `ashar	السـابـع عـشـر
18th	ath thaamin `ashar	الثـامـن عـشـر
19th	at taa si` `ashar	التـاسـع عـشـر
20th	al`ishruun	العـشـرون
21st	alhaadii wal `ishruun	الحـادي والـعـشـرون
22nd	ath thaanii wal `ishruun	الثاني والعشرون
23rd	ath thaalith wal `ishruun	الثاني والعشرون
24th	arraabi` wal `ishruun	الرابـع والعشرون
25th	alkhaamis wal `ishruun	الـخامس والعشرون
26th	assaadis wal `ishruun	السادس والعشرون
27th	assaabi` wal `ishruun	السابع العشرون

28th	ath-thaamin wal `ishruun	الثامن والعشرون
29th	attaasi` wal `ishruun	التاسع والعشرون
30th	ath-thalaathuun	الثلاثون
31st	alhaadii wath-thalaathuun	الحادي والثلاثون

What day of the month is this?

maa taariikhul yawwm? ما تاريخ اليوم؟

It's the 5th. alkhaamis الخامس

Tomorrow will be the 6th.

ghadan sayakuunus saadis غداً سيكون السادس

I was born on July 27th.

wulidtu fis saabi` wal `ishriin min yuulyu

ولدت في السابع والعشرين من يوليو

Tomorrow will be the 20th of June.

ghadan sayakuunul `ishriin min yuunyu

غداً سيكون العشرين من يونيو

I am leaving on the 14th of May.

sa'ughaadiru fir raabi` ashar min maayu

سأغادر في الرابع من مايو

I want these documents by the 20th of August.

'uriidu tilkal wathaa'iq qablal `ishriin min 'ughustus

أريد هذه الوثائق قبل العشرين من أغسطس

Years

year	sanah/`aam	سنة/عـام
this year	haadhihis sanah	هذه السنة
last year	assanah almaadiyah	السنة الماضية
next year	assanah alqaadimah	السنة القادمة
every year	kul sanah	كل سنة
new year	sanah jadiidah	سنة جديدة
for one year	li`aam	لعـام
year and a half	`aam wa nisf	عـام ونصف
for three years	lithalaathati a`waam	لثلاثة أعوام
Happy New Year	`aam sa`iid	عـام سعيـد
New Year's Eve	laylat ra's as-sanah	ليلة رأس السنة

I have studied Arabic for two years.
darastu al`arabiyyah li`aamayn
درست العـربيـة لعـامـين

I came to Syria this year.
ji'tu 'ilaa suuryaa haadhal `aam
جئت إلى سوريا هذا العـام

I was there last year.
kuntu hunaak al`aam almaadii
كنت هناك العـام الماضي

Happy anniversary!
kul aam wa anta bi khayr!   كل عـام وأنت بخيـر!

1970	'alf wa tatis'u mi'ah wa sab'uun
	ألف وتسعمائة وسبعون
1980	'alf wa tatis'u mi'ah wa thamaanuun
	ألف وتسعمائة وثمانون
1990	'alf wa tatis'u mi'ah wa tis'uun
	ألف وتسعمائة وتسعون
1995	'alf wa tatis'u mi'ah wa khamsah wa tis'uun
	ألف وتسعمائة وخمسة وتسعون
2000	'alfaan ألفان
2001	'alfaan wa waahid ألفان وواحد
2002	'alfaan wa ithnaan ألفان واثنان
2003	'alfaan wa thalaathah ألفان وثلاثة
2004	'alfaan wa arba'ah ألفان وأربعة
2005	'alfaan wa khamsah ألفان وخمسة
2006	'alfaan wa sittah ألفان وستة
2007	'alfaan wa sab'ah ألفان وسبعة
2008	'alfaan wa thamaaniyah ألفان وثمانية
2009	'alfaan wa tis'ah ألفان وتسعة
2010	'alfaan wa 'asharah ألفان وعشرة

I was born in 1974.

wulidtu fii `aam alf wa tis` mi'ah wa arba`ah wa sab`iin

ولدت في عام ألف وتسعمائة وأربعة وسبعين

I have been working for this company since August 2004.

a`malu fii haadhihish sharikah mundhu`ughustus `aam alfayyn wa arba`ah

أعمل في هذه الشركة منذ أغسطس عام
ألفين وأربعة

Seasons

season	faṣl	فـصـل
winter	shitaa'	شـتـاء
spring	rabii`	ربـيـع
summer	ṣayf	صـيـف
autumn	khariif	خـريـف

What is the best season in Syria?
maa huwa afḍalu al-fuṣuul fii suuryaa?
مـا هـو أفـضـل الـفـصول فـي سـوريـا؟

When does summer begin?
mataa yabda'uṣ ṣayf? مـتى يـبـدأ الصـيـف؟

Is it very cold during winter?
haliṭ ṭaqṣu baaridun jiddan athnaa'a ash-shitaa'?
هـل الطـقـس بـارد جـداً أثـنـاء الـشـتاء؟

What is the high temperature in Riyadh?
maa hiya darajat ḥaraarah alquṣwaa fii ar-riyaad?
مـا هـي درجـة الـحـرارة الـقـصـوى فـي الـريـاض؟

Time

hour	saa`ah	سـاعـة
minute	daqiiqah	دقـيـقـة

second	<u>th</u>aaniyah	ثانية
midnight	munta<u>s</u>af layl	منتصف ليل
a.m.	sabaa<u>h</u>an	صباحاً
p.m.	masaa'an	مساءً
early	mubakkir	مبكّر
late	muta'a<u>kh</u>-<u>kh</u>ir	متأخّر
appointment	maw`id	موعد
before	qabla	قبل
after	ba`da	بعد
during	'a<u>th</u>naa'	أثناء
noon	<u>z</u>uhr	ظهر

What time is it? kam as-saa`ah? كم الساعة؟

It is 1 o'clock now.
assaa`atu al'aan alwaa<u>h</u>idah الساعة الآن الواحدة

2 o'clock	a<u>th</u>-<u>th</u>aaniyah	الثانية
3 o'clock	a<u>th</u>-<u>th</u>aali<u>th</u>ah	الثالثة
4 o'clock	arraabi`ah	الرابعة
5 o'clock	al<u>kh</u>aamisah	الخامسة
6 o'clock	assaadisah	السادسة
7 o'clock	assaabi`ah	السابعة
8 o'clock	a<u>th</u>-<u>th</u>aaminah	الثامنة
9 o'clock	at-taasi`ah	التاسعة
10 o'clock	al-`aa<u>sh</u>irah	العاشرة
11 o'clock	alhaadiyata `a<u>sh</u>rata	الحادية عشرة
12 o'clock	a<u>th</u>-<u>th</u>aaniyata `a<u>sh</u>rata	الثانية عشرة
five past one	alwaa<u>h</u>idah wa <u>kh</u>ams daqaa'iq	
		الواحدة وخمس دقائق

ten past two	ath-thaaniyah wa `ashr daqaa'iq الثانية وعشر دقائق
quarter past five	alkhaamisah war-rub` الخامسة والربع
twenty past two	ath-thaaniyah wath-thuluth الثانية والثلث
half past seven	assaabi`ah wan nisf السابعة والنصف
quarter to nine	at-taasi`ah 'illa rub` التاسعة إلا ربع
twenty to ten	al`aashirah 'illa thulth العاشرة إلا ثلث
ten to eleven	alhaadiyata `ashrata 'illaa `ashr daqaa'iq الحادية عشرة إلا عشر دقائق

1 minute	daqiiqah دقيقة
2 minutes	daqiiqataan دقيقتان
3 minutes	thalaath daqaa'iq ثلاث دقائق
4 minutes	arba` daqaa'iq أربع دقائق
5 minutes	khams daqaa'iq خمس دقائق
6 minutes	sitt daqaa'iq ست دقائق
7 minutes	sab` daqaa'iq سبع دقائق
8 minutes	thamaan daqaa'iq ثمان دقائق
9 minutes	tis` daqaa'iq تسع دقائق
10 minutes	`ashr daqaa'iq عشر دقائق
quarter of an hour	rub` saa`ah ربع ساعة
half an hour	nisf saa`ah نصف ساعة
an hour	saa`ah ساعة
an hour and a half	saa`ah wa nisf ساعة ونصف
2 hours	saa`ataan ساعتان
3 hours	thalaath saa`aat ثلاث ساعات
4 hours	arba` saa`aat أربع ساعات
5 hours	khams saa`aat خمس ساعات
6 hours	sit saa`aat ست ساعات

7 hours	sab' saa`aat	سبع ساعات
8 hours	thamaanii saa`aat	ثماني ساعات
9 hours	tis` saa`aat	تسع ساعات
10 hours	ashr saa`aat	عشر ساعات
24 hours	'arba` wa `ishruun saa `ah	أربع وعشرون ساعة
36 hours	sittah wa thalaathuun saa`ah	ستة وثلاثون ساعة
72 hours	ithnaan wa sab`uun saa`ah	اثنان وسبعون ساعة

What time is it now? kamis saa`atol aan? كم الساعة الآن؟

What time are we leaving?
mataa sanughaadir? متى سنغادر؟

What time does the bus leave?
mataa yughaadirul baas? متى يغادر الباص؟

What time is breakfast? matal 'iftaar? متى الإفطار؟

What time is lunch? matal ghadaa'? متى الغداء؟

What time is dinner? matal `ashaa'? متى العشاء؟

One moment, please!
lahzah min fadlik! لحظة من فضلك!

What time does the museum open?
mataa yaftahul muthaf? متى يفتح المتحف؟

What time does the movie start?
mataa yabda'ul film? متـى يبدأ الـفيلـم ؟

Are you busy after 7:00 p.m.?
hal 'anta mashghuul ba`das saabi`ah?
هـل أنـت مـشـغـول بـعـد الـسـابـعـة؟

Yes, I am. na`am 'anaa mashghuul نـعـم أنـا مـشـغـول

What time is departure?
matal mughaadarah? متـى الـمـغـادرة؟

It is at 5:30 a.m.
fil khaamisati wannisf sabaahan
فـي الـخـامـسـة والـنـصف صبـاحـاً

What time is your appointment?
mataa maw`iduk? متـى مـوعـدك؟

Will this take a long time?
hal saya'khudhu dhaalika waqtan tawiilan?
هـل سـيـأخـذ ذلك وقـتـاً طـويـلاً؟

I think it will take about half an hour.
'azunnu 'annahu saya'khudh nisf saa`ah taqriiban
أظن أنه سيأخذ نصف ساعة تقريباً

I will be back shortly. sa `auudu qariiban سـأعـود قـريـبـاً

I will be back in 10 minutes.
sa 'a`uudu ba`da `ashri daqaa'iq
سـأعـود بـعـد عـشـر دقائق

I will try to finish it in an hour.
sa 'uhaawilu an antahiya minh fii saa`ah
سـأحـاول أن أنـتـهـي مـنـه فـي ساعـة

If I have time, I would like to go to Aleppo.
'arghabu fidh-dhahaabi `ilaa halab `idhaa kaana `indii waqt
أرغـب فـي الذهـاب إلـى حـلـب إذا كـان عـنـدي وقـت

It's late, isn't it?
alwaqtu muta`akh-khir, `alayysa kadhaalik?
الـوقـت مـتـأخـر، أليـس كـذلـك؟

It is still early.
alwaqtu laa yazaalu mubakkiran   الـوقـت لا يـزال مـبـكـراً

Sorry, I am late.
'aasif anaa muta`akh- khir   آسـف أنـا مـتـأخـر

The Weather

temperature	darajat al-haraarah درجـة الـحـرارة	
weather forecast	annashrah al-jawwiyyah النـشـرة الـجـويـة	
cold	baarid بـارد	

hot	haarr	حـارّ
moderate	mu`tadil	مـعـتـدل
changing (adj.)	mutaqallib	متقلّب
humid	ratib	رطـب
dry	jaaff	جـافّ
wind	riih	ريـح
storm	aasifah	عـاصـفـة
rain	matar	مـطـر
rainy	maatir	مـاطـر
snow	thalj	ثلـج
freezing (adj.)	mutajammid	متجمّـد
jacket	mi`taf	مـعـطـف
gloves	quffaazaat	قـفـازات
umbrella	mizallah	مـظـلّـة
sunglasses	nazzaarah shamsiyyah	نظارة شمسية
hat	qubba`ah	قـبـعـة

What is the weather like today?
kayfa huwat taqsul yawm?   كيف هو الـطـقـس الـيـوم؟

It is hot. `innahu haarr   إنـه حـارّ

It is cold. `innahu baarid   إنـه بـارد

Where can I buy a raincoat?
ayna yumkinunii `an `ashtarii mi`taf matar?
أيـن يـمـكـنـني أن أشـتـري مـعـطـف مـطـر؟

I don't like humid weather.
laa `uhibbul jawwar ratib   لا أحـب الـجـوّ الـرطـب

Will it rain tonight?
hal satumṭirul layylah? هـل سـتـمـطـر الـلـيـلـة؟

It's raining outside.
'innahaa tumṭiru fil khaarij إنّـها تمطر في الخارج

It's raining heavily.
'innahaa tumṭiru bi ghazaarah إنـها تـمـطـر بغزارة

Do I need an umbrella?
hal sa'aḥtaaju 'ilaa miẓallah? هـل سـأحـتـاج إلـى مـظـلـة؟

Money

money	nuquud	نـقـود
currency	`umlah	عُـمـلـة
Australian dollar	dulaar 'usturaaliyy	دولار أسـتـرالـيّ
British pound sterling	junayh istarliiniyy	
		جنـيـه استـرلـيـنـي
Egyptian pound	junayh miṣriyy	جنـيـه مصـري
Jordanian dinar	diinaar 'urduniyy	ديـنـار أردني
Saudi riyal	riyaal su`uudiyy	ريـال سعـودي
Syrian lira	liirah suuriyyah	لـيـرة سـوريـة
UAE dirham	dirham imaaraatiyy	درهم إمـاراتـي
U.S. dollar	dulaar 'amriikiyy	دولار أمـريـكـيّ
money exchange	taṣriif `umlah	تصـريـف عمـلـة
traveler's check	shiik siyaaḥiyy	شيـك سيـاحـي
credit card	biṭaaqat i'timaan	بـطـاقـة ائـتـمـان

cash	naqdan	نـقـداً
expensive	ghaalin غالٍ (commonly used as غالي ghaalii)	
cheap	rakhiis	رخـيـص
budget	miizaaniyyah	مـيـزانيـة

What is the exchange rate for the U.S. dollar today?
maa huwa si`r sarf addulaar al'amriikiyy alyawm?
مـا هـو سـعـر صـرف الـدولار الأمـريـكـي الـيـوم؟

How much are these in local currency?
kam haadhal mablagh bil `umlah almahalliyahh?
كـم هـذا الـمـلـغ بـالـعـمـلـة الـمـحـلـيـة؟

Would you please change 100 U.S. dollars into UAE dirham?
momkin an tuhawwil mi'at dulaar amriikiyy `ilaa dirham
imaaraatiyy?
مـمـكـن أن تـحـول مـائـة درهـم أمـريـكـي إلـى درهـم
أمـاراتـي؟

Do you have change for 20 dinar?
`indak fakkat `ishriin diinaar?
عـنـدك فـكـة عـشـريـن ديـنـار؟

My budget is 3000 riyals.
miizaaniyyatii thalaathat aalaaf riyaal
مـيـزانـيـتـي ثـلاثـة آلاف ريـال

This is a little expensive.
haadhaa ghalin qaliilan هـذا غـالٍ قـلـيـلا

Could you give me a cheaper rate?
mumkin an tu`tiinii si`r afdal?
ممكن أن تـعطيني سـعراً أفضل؟

In the Restaurant

food	ta`aam	طـعـام
Arabian food	ta`aam `arabiyy	طـعـام عـربـيّ
Western food	ta`aam gharbiyy	طـعـام غـربـيّ
cafeteria	maqsaf	مـقصـف
dining room	ghurfat ta`aam	غـرفـة طـعـام
coffee shop	maqhaa	مـقـهـى
fast food	wajbah sarii`ah	وجـبـة سـريـعـة
food delivery	tawsiil lil manaazil	توصيل للمنازل
menu	qaa'imat ta`aam	قـائـمـة طـعـام
meat	lahm	لـحـم
chicken	dajaaj	دجـاج
fish	samak	سـمـك
seafood	'aklaat bahriyyah	أكـلات بـحـريـة
vegetables	khudaar	خـضـار
hummus	hummus	حـمـص
fruits	fawaakih	فـواكـه
sugar	sukkar	سـكّـر
salt	milh	مـلـح
pepper	fulful	فـلـفـل
rice	'aruzz	أرزّ
soup	hasaa` /shurbah	شـوربـة /حـسـاء
meal	wajbah	وجـبـة

main dish	ṭabaq ra'iisii طبق رئيسي
side dish	ṭabaq jaanibii طبق جانبي
dessert	ḥalwaa حلوى
ice cream	muthallajaat مثلجات (commonly used as it is in English)
drink (n.)	mashruub مشروب
water	maa' ماء
boiling water	maa' maghliyy ماء مغليّ
cold water	maa' baarid ماء بارد
tea	shaay شاي
iced tea	shay muthallaj شاي مثلج
coffee	qahwah قهوة
black coffee	qahwah saadah قهوة سادة
coffee without sugar	qahwah murrah قهوة مرّة
coffee with sugar	qahwah ḥulwah قهوة حلوة
coffee with milk	qahwah bil-ḥaliib قهوة بالحليب
milk	ḥaliib حليب
juice	'aṣiir عصير
orange juice	'aṣiir burtuqaal عصير برتقال
lemon juice	'aṣiir laymuun عصير ليمون
apple juice	'aṣiir tuffaaḥ عصير تفاح
banana juice	'aṣiir mawz عصير موز
mineral water	miyaah ma'daniyyah مياه معدنيّة
soft drink	mashruub ghaaziyy مشروب غازيّ
alcoholic drink	mashruub kuḥuuliyy مشروب كحوليّ
beer	biirah بيرة
wine	nabiidh نبيذ

table	ṯaawilah	طاولة
knife	sikkiin	سكين
fork	shawwkah	شوكة
spoon	mil`aqah	ملعقة
plate	ṣaḥn	صحن
toothpick	nakkaashat asnaan	نكاشة أسنان
napkin	mindiil	منديل
tray	ṣiiniyyah	صينية
soap	ṣaabuun	صابون
hot	ḥaarr	حارّ
cold	baarid	بارد
warm	daafi'	دافئ
delicious	ladhiidh لذيذ/zaakii زاكي (common in Syria, Lebanon, Palestine and Jordan)	
not delicious	ghayr ladhiidh	غير لذيذ
sweet	hulw	حلو
salty	maaliḥ	مالح

I am hungry. ana jaa'i` أنا جائع

Do you have a menu in English?
hal `indaka qaa'imat ta`aam bil inkliiziyyah?
هل عندك قائمة طعام بالإنجليزية؟

What do you want to eat?
maadhaa turiidu an ta'kul? ماذا تريد أن تأكل؟

What time do you eat? mataa ta'kul? متى تأكل؟

Let's go out and eat something.
falnadh-hab lina'kula shay'an فلنذهب لنأكل شيئاً

I like Arabian food.
'uhibbut ta'aama al'arabiyy أحب الطعام العربيّ

A table for two, please.
taawilah li shakhsayn law samaht
طاولة لشخصين لو سمحت

A menu, please.
qaa'imat atta'aam law samaht
قائمة الطعام لو سمحت

What is this meal called?
masmu haadhihil wajbah? ما اسم هذه الوجبة ؟

Please bring me... .
'arjuu an tuhdira lii... . ... أرجو أن تحضرلي

I would like to eat... .
'awaddu an 'aakola ... . أود أن آكل

More salt and pepper please.
almaziid minal milh walbihaaraat law samaht
المزيد من الملح والبهارات لو سمحت

Is that enough? hal haadhaa yakfii? هل هذا يكفي؟

Please give me a little more.
'arjuu an tu`tiinii akthar qaliilan
أرجو أن تـعـطـنـي أكـثر قـلـيـلاً

That is enough. haadhaa kaafin هـذا كـافٍ

That is too much. haadhaa kathiir هـذا كـثـيـر

I cannot eat all of this.
laa astatii`u an 'aakula kulla haadhaa
لا أستـطـيـع أن آكـل كـل هـذا

Thanks for the delicious meal.
shukran `alal wajbah alladhiidhah
شـكـراً عـلـى الـوجـبـة الـلـذيـذة

I am thirsty. anaa `atshaan أنـا عـطـشـان

What do you want to drink?
madhaa turiidu an tashrab? مـاذا تـريـد أن تـشـرب ؟

I will have coffee, please.
sa'aakhudhu qahwah law samaht سآخـذ قـهوة لـو سـمـحـت

I will have black coffee, please.
sa'aakhudhu qahwah saadah law samaht
سآخـذ قـهوة سـادة لـو سـمـحـت

More coffee, please.

almaziid minal qahwah law sama<u>h</u>t

المزيد من القهوة لو سمحت

I will have tea with milk, please.

sa'aa<u>kh</u>udhu <u>sh</u>aay ma`a <u>h</u>aliib law sama<u>h</u>t

سآخذ شاي مع حليب لو سمحت

Tea with lemon, please.

<u>sh</u>ay ma` laymuun law sama<u>h</u>t

شاي مع ليمون لو سمحت

A glass of milk, please.

kuuba <u>h</u>aliib, law sama<u>h</u>t كوب حليب لو سمحت

A bottle of mineral water, please.

qaaruurat miyaah ma`daniyyah, law sama<u>h</u>t

قارورة مياه معدنيّة لو سمحت

Yes, please. na`am, min fa<u>d</u>lik نعم، من فضلك

No, thank you. laa, <u>sh</u>ukran لا، شكراً

The bill, please.

alfaatuurah min fa<u>d</u> lik الفاتورة من فضلك

Paying Bills

bill	faatuurah / hisaab حِساب / فَاتورة
receipt	wasl وَصل
cash	naqdan نَقداً
credit card	bitaaqat i'timaan بِطاقة ائتمان

The bill, please. alhisaab min fadlik الحِساب مِن فَضلِك

A separate bill, please.
hisaab munfasil law samaht
حِساب مُنفَصِل لو سَمَحت

How much is it altogether?
kamil hisaab bel kaamil? كَم الحِساب بِالكامِل؟

Do you accept credit cards?
hal taqbal bitaaqaat i'timaan?
هَل تَقبَل بِطاقات ائتمان؟

Can I pay by credit card?
mumkin 'an 'adfa' bibitaaqatil i'timaan?
مُمكِن أن أدفَع بِبِطاقة الائتمان؟

A receipt, please. alwasl min fadlik الوَصل مِن فَضلِك

Locating Toilets

men's toilet	<u>h</u>ammaam rijaal	حمام رجال
women's toilet	<u>h</u>ammaam sayyidaat	حمام سيدات
public toilet	<u>h</u>ammaam `umuumiyy	حمام عمومّي
washroom	ma<u>gh</u>aasil	مغاسل

Is there a toilet here?

hal yuujad <u>h</u>ammaam hunaa? هل يوجد حمام هنا؟

Where is the toilet please?

aynal <u>h</u>ammaam min fa<u>d</u>lik? أين الحمّام من فضلك؟

Is there a nearby public toilet?

hal yuujadu <u>h</u>ammaam `umuumiyy qariib?
هل يوجد حمّام عمومي قريب؟

I need to go to the toilet.

a<u>h</u>taaju an a<u>dh</u>-haba ilal <u>h</u>ammaam
أحتاج أن أذهب إلى الحمّام

May I use the toilet please?

mumkin an asta<u>kh</u>dimal <u>h</u>ammaam min fa<u>d</u>lik?
ممكن أن أستخدم الحمام من فضلك؟

At the Airport

airplane	ṭaa'irah طائـرة
airplane ticket	tadhkirat ṭayaraan تذكرة طيران
reservations	ḥajz حـجـز
first class	darajah 'uulaa درجـة أولـى
economy class	darajah siyaaḥiyyah درجـة سيـاحيـة
reservation confirmation	ta'kiid al-ḥajz تأكيـد الحجـز
passport	jawaaz safar جـواز سفـر
terminal	qaa`at al'intiẓaar قاعة انتظـار
gate	bawwaabah بـوّابـة
customs	jamaarik جمـارك
inspection	taftiish تفتيـش
arrivals	alqaadimuun الـقـادمـون
departures	almughaadiruun الـمـغـادرون
window seat	maq`ad mujaawir lish-shubbaak مقـعـد مجـاورللـشـبّاك
luggage	amti`ah أمتعة
travel agency	wakaalat ṭayaraan وكالة طيران
pilot	ṭayyaar طيّـار
flight attendant (fem.)	muḍiifat ṭayaraan مضيفـة طيـران

Two tickets to Dubai, please.
tadhkaratayn `ilaa dubay min faḍlik
تـذكـرتـيـن إلـى دبي مـن فـضـلـك

Where is the airport? 'aynal maṭaar? أيـن المطـار؟

What time does the Cairo plane land?

mataa taṣilu ṭaa'iratul qaahirah?

متى ستصل طائرة القاهرة؟

To the airport, please.

'ilal maṭaar min faḏlik   إلى المطار من فضلك

How long does it take to reach the airport?

kam minal waqti naḥtaaju linaṣila 'ilal maṭaar?

كم من الوقت نحتاج لنصل إلى المطار؟

Please meet me at the airport.

qaabilnii fil maṭaar min faḏlik

قابلني في المطار من فضلك

I will be at the airport.

sa'akuunu fil maṭaar   سأكون في المطار

Will you come to pick me up from the airport?

hal sata'tii lita'khudhanii minal maṭaar?

هل ستأتي لتأخذني من المطار؟

I will pick you up from the airport.

sa 'aakhudhuka minal maṭaar   سأخذك من المطار

I will call you from the airport.

sa 'attaṣilu bika minal maṭaar   سأتصل بك من المطار

Is there an international airport?

hal yuujadu maṭaar dawliyy?   هل يوجد مطار دولي؟

Shopping

shopping center/mall	markaz tasawwuq
	مركز تسوّق
shop	mahal/dukkaan محل / دكان
gift shop	mahal hadaayaa محل هدايا
grocery	baqqaalah بقالة
bookstore	maktabah مكتبة
antiques	tuhaf تحف
souvenirs	tadhkaar تذكار
greeting cards	bitaaqaat tahni'ah
	بطاقة تهنئة
poster	mulsaq ملصق
book	kitaab كتاب
clothes	malaabis ملابس
jewelry	mujawharaat مجوهرات
accessories	kamaaliyyah كماليات
toys	'al`aab ألعاب
watches	saa`aat ساعات
leather	jild جلد
tourist map	khariitat suyyaah
	خريطة سياح
English-Arabic dictionary	qaamuus inkliiziyy `arabiyy
	قاموس إنجليزيّ عربيّ
birthday	`iid miilaad عيد ميلاد
Christmas	`iid al-miilaad al-majiid
	عيد الميلاد المجيد
wedding anniversary	dhikraa zawaaj ذكرى زواج
Mother's Day	`iidul `umm عيد الأمّ
Father's Day	`iidul `ab عيد الأب

Valentine's Day	`iid alhub	عيد الحـب
how much	bikam	بكم
discount	khasm	خصم
expensive	ghaalii	غالي
cheap	rakhiis	رخيص
large/big	kabiir	كبير
small	saghiir	صغير
tight	dayyiq	ضيق

I will buy... . sa `ashtarii ساشتري

I want to buy... . `uriidu an ashtarii... . ...أريد أن أشتري

I would like to buy it. awaddu `an `ashtariih أود أن أشتريه

I bought it. ishtaraytuh اشتريته

I am not going to buy it. lan `ashtariih لن أشتريه

Did you buy it? halish taraytah? هل اشتريته؟

How much did you buy it for?
bikamish taraytah? بكم اشتريته؟

Who bought it? manish taraah? من اشتراه؟

What do you want to buy?
maadhaa turiid an tash tarii? ماذا تريد أن تشتري؟

Where did you buy that from?
min aynash taaraytah?   من أين اشتريته؟

What did you buy? maadhash tarayt?   ماذا اشتريت؟

Is there a shopping center nearby?
hal yuujadu markazu tasawwuqin qariib?
هـل يـوجـد مـركـز تـسـوّق قـريـب؟

How much is this in U.S. dollars?
bikam haadhaa biddulaar al'amriikiyy?
بـكـم هـذا بـالـدولار الأمـريـكـي؟

I am just browsing. 'ana 'atafarraj faqat   أنـا أتفـرّج فـقـط

I would like a pair of shoes, please.
'awaddu shiraa'a zawj 'ahdhiyah law samaht
أودّ شـراء زوج أحـذيـة لـو سـمـحـت

I need some razor blades.
'ahtaaju 'ilaa shafraat   أحـتـاج إلـى شـفـرات

I need some sanitary napkins.
'ahtaaju 'ilaa manadiil.   أحـتـاج إلـى مـنـاديـل

I am looking for... .
'ana 'abhathu `an... .   ... أنـا أبـحـث عـن

How much is this? bikam haadhaa?   بـكـم هـذا؟

I want that jacket.

'uriidu dhaalikal mi'ṭaf   أريد ذلك المعطف

May I have a receipt?

alwaṣl law samaḥt?   الوصل لو سمحت؟

Do you accept Australian dollars?

hal taqbalu dulaaraat 'usturaaliyyah?
هل تقبل دولارات أسرالية؟

I want to buy a present for my wife.

'uriidu an ashtarii hadiyyatan li zawjatii
أريد أن أشتري هدية لزوجتي

Please show me... .

'uriidu 'an turiyanii... .   ...أريد أن تريني

May I see that... ?

hal yumkinunii 'an 'araa dhaalik al... ?
هل يمكنني أن أرى ذلك .... ؟

I want to buy it. 'uriidu an'ashtariih   أريد أن أشتريه

What is the price, please?

maa huwas si'r min faḍlik?   ما هو السعر من فضلك؟

How much does this cost?

kam yukallifu haadhaa?   كم يكلف هذا؟

Is the price negotiable?

halis si`r qaabil littafaawud?

هل السعر قابل للتفاوض؟

Are prices fixed here?

hal al-as`aar thaabitah hunaa?

هل الأسعار ثابتة هنا؟

This is very expensive.

haadhaa ghaalii jiddan

هذا غالي جدّاً

This is very cheap.

haadhaa rakhiis jiddan

هذا رخيص جدّاً

Public Transportation

bus	haafilah; *baas**	حافلة ، باص
bus stop/stand	mawqif albaas	موقف الباص
bus depot	mujamma` albaasaat	مُجمَّع الباصات
driver	saa'iq	سائق

* haafilah is the proper word for "bus" but *baas* is so common that it can be used.

train	qitaar	قطار
train station	mahattat qitaar	محطة قطار
railway	sikak hadiidiyyah	سكك حديدية
express train	qitaar sari`	قطار سريع
steam train	qitaar sarii`	قطار بخاري
ticket officer	muwazzaf attadhaakir	موظف التذاكِر

ticket office	maktab attadhaakir	مـكـتـب الـتـذاكـر
one-way ticket	tadhkarat dhahaab	تـذكـرة ذهـاب
return ticket	tadhkarat 'iyaab	تـذكـرة إيـاب
schedule	jadwal	جدول
timetable	jadwal `amal	جدول عمل
get on	yas`ad 'ilaa	يـصـعـد إلـى
get off	yanzil min	يـنـزل مـن

Is there a nearby bus stop?
hal yuujadu mawqifu baasaat qariibun min hunaa?
هـل يـوجـد مـوقـف بـاصـات قـريـب مـن هـنا؟

Where is the bus station?
'ayna mahattat albaasat? أيـن مـحـطـة الـبـاصـات؟

How can I get to the bus station?
kayfa yumkinunii 'an 'adh-haba `ilaa mahattatil baas?
كـيـف يـمـكـن أن أذهـب إلـى مـحـطـة الـبـاصـات؟

Which bus should I take to go to Hamidiyya Market?
'ayyu baas yajibu 'an 'aakhudha li'adh-haba `ilaa suuqil hami-
idiyyah?
أي بـاص يـجـب أن آخـذ لأذهـب إلـى سـوق الـحـمـيـديـة؟

What is the busfare? kam `ujratul baas? كـم هـي أجـرة الباص؟

Do you have the bus schedule/timetable?
hal ladayka jadwal `amal al-baasaat?
هـل لـديـك جـدول عـمـل الـبـاصـات؟

Where does the downtown bus leave from?

min 'ayna yanṭaliq albaaṣ almutawajjih 'ilaa markazil madiinah?

من أين ينطلق الباص المتجه إلى مركز المدينة؟

Is there a bus that goes to the airport?

hal hunaaka baaṣ yadh-habu 'ilal maṭaar?

هل هناك باص يذهب إلى المطار؟

Where is the train station?

'ayna maḥaṭṭatul qiṭaar?   أين محطة القطار؟

I want to go to Cairo by train.

'uriidu 'an 'adh-haba 'ilal qaahirah bil qiṭaar

أريد أن أذهب إلى القاهرة بالقطار

Where should I get on the train that goes to… ?

min 'ayna 'aakhudhul qiṭaaral mutawajjih 'ilaa … ?

من أين آخذ القطار المتوجه إلى...؟

How can I go to the train station?

kayfa adh-habu `ilaa maḥaṭṭatil qiṭaar?

كيف أذهب إلى محطة القطار؟

Please take me to the train station.

arjuu an ta'khudhanii `ilaa maḥaṭṭatil qiṭaar

أرجو أن تأخذني إلى محطة القطار

Where can I buy a ticket?

min ayna yumkinunii an ashtarii tadhkarah?

من أين يمكنني أن أشتري تذكرة؟

How much is the train ticket?

bikam tadhkaratul qitaar?   بكم تذكرة القطار؟

Visiting an Office

businessman	rajul a`maal	رجل أعمال
businesswoman	sayyidat 'a`maal	سيِّدة أعمال
business hours	saa`aat addawaam arrasmiyy	ساعات الدوام الرسمي
company	sharikah	شركة
institution	mu'assasah	مؤسسة
office	maktab	مكتب
factory	masna`	مصنع
director	mudiir	مدير
employee	muwazzaf	موظف
employer	saahib `amal	صاحب عمل
profession	hirfah	حرفة
career	mihnah	مهنة
job	waziifah	وظيفة
conference room	qaa`at mu'tamaraat	قاعة مؤتمرات
meeting	ijtimaa`	اجتماع
invitation	da`wah	دعوة
capital (money)	ra's maal	رأس مال

consultant	mustashaar	مستشار
distributor	muwazzi`	موزع
president	ra'iis	رئيس
vice president	naa'ib arra'iis	نائب الرئيس
representative	mumath-thil	ممثل
contract	`aqd	عقد
telephone	haatif	هاتف
fax	faaks	فاكس
address	`unwaan	عنوان
E-mail	bariid 'iliktruniyy	بريد إلكتروني

Where do you work? 'ayna ta`mal? أين تعمل؟

I work in... . 'anaa 'a`malu fii... . أنا أعمل في.......

What time does the conference start?
mataa tabda'ul mu'tamar? متى يبدأ المؤتمر؟

Please meet me at the hotel.
'arjuu 'an tuqaabilanii fil funduq
أرجو أن تقابلني في الفندق

I have an important meeting.
`indii ijtimaa`un muhim عندي اجتماع مهم

What time shall I come?
mataa yajibu 'an 'aatii? متى يجب أن آتي؟

What time does the meeting start?
mataa yabda'ul ijtimaa`? متى يبدأ الاجتماع؟

I am sorry to be late.

'aasif 'ana muta'akh-khir   آسف، أنا متأخّر

What is the name of your company?

masmu sharikatik?   ما اسم شركتك؟

Where is your office? 'ayna maktabuk?   أين مكتبك؟

What is your address? maa `unwaanuk?   ما عنوانك؟

What is your telephone number?

maa raqmu haatifik?   ما رقم هاتفك؟

Would you please write it down?

sajjilhu lii law samaht?   سجله لي لو سمحت

I will give you a call. sa'attasil bik   سأتصل بك

Would you please call me?

ittasil bii min fadlik?   اتصل بي من فضلك

I would like to meet Mr. Abdullah.

'awaddu 'an `uqaabil assayyid `abdallah

أود أن أقابل السيد عبد الله

When can I meet Mr. Ahmed?

mataa yumkinunii 'an `uqaabilas sayyid `ahmad?

متى يمكنني أن أقابل السيد أحمد؟

Will 2 p.m. tomorrow be okay?

hal assaa`ah ath-thaaniyah ghadan ma saa'an waqtun munaasib?

هل الساعة الثانية غداً مساء وقت مناسب؟

Yes, that will be fine with me.

na`am haadhaa yunaasibunii نعم هذا يناسبني

I have an appointment with Mr. Mohammad at 10 a.m.

`indii maw`id ma`as sayyid Muhammad assaa`ah al`aashirah sabaahan

عندي موعد مع السيد محمد الساعة العاشرة صباحاً

Where will the meeting be held?

`ayna sayu`qadul ijtimaa`? أين سيُعقد الاجتماع؟

Would you please tell him that I have arrived? My name is Paolo.

mumkin an taquul lahu annii qad wasalt? ismii baawlu

ممكن أن تقول له أني قد وصلت؟ اسمي باولو

Yes, he is expecting me. We have an appointment.

na`am huwa yantazirunii, ladaynnaa maw`id

نعم هو ينتظرني، لدينا موعد

Can I use your telephone?

mumkin 'an 'asta`mila haatifak?

ممكن أن أستعمل هاتفك؟

Can I wait here?

mumkin 'an 'antazira hunaa? ممكن أن أنتظر هنا؟

At the Post Office

mail	bariid	بـريـد
mail (v.)	yursil bil bariid	يـرسل بـالـبـريـد
post office	maktab bariid	مكتب بـريـد
post officer	saa`ii bariid	ساعـي الـبـريـد
postcard	biṯaaqah bariidiyyah	بطـاقـه بـريـديـة
airmail	bariid jawwiyy	بريد جـوّيَ
express mail	bariid musta`jal	بـريـد مـسـتـعـجـل
registered mail	bariid musajjal	بـريـد مـسـجـل
letter	risaalah	رسـالـة
postal address	`unwaan bariidiyy	عنوان بـريـدي
P.O. box	ṣunduuq bariid	صـنـدوق بـريـد
stamp	ṯaabi`	طـابـع
envelope	ẓarf	ظـرف
send	yursil	يـرسـل
receive	yastalim	يـستـلـم

Where is the nearest post office?
`ayna `aqrabu maktabi bariid?   أيـن أقـرب مـكتـب بـريـد؟

How do I get to the post office?
kayfa `aṣilu `ilaa maktabil bariid?
كـيـف أصـل إلـى مـكتـب الـبـريـد؟

What time does the post office open?
mataa yaftaḥu maktabul bariid?
متـى يـفتـح مكتب الـبـريـد؟

I need a stamp. 'ahtaaju 'ilaa taabi' أحتاج إلى طابع

I would like to send this to the U.S. by airmail.
'awaddu 'an 'ursilahu 'ilaa 'amriikaa bil bariid aljawwiyy
أود أن أرسله إلى أمريكا بالبريد بالبريد الجويّ

How long will it take for this shipment to reach the U.K.?
mataa tasilu haadhihish shuhnah 'ilaa briitaanyaa?
متى تصل هذه الشحنة إلى بريطانيا؟

Medical Emergency

emergency room	ghurfat tawaari'	غرفة طوارئ
registration, reception	al-istiqbaal	الاستقبال
accident	haadith	حادث
nurse (fem.)	mumarridah	ممرضة
operation	'amaliyyah	عملية
patient	mariid	مريض
pharmacy	sayydaliyyah	صيدليّة
pharmacist	saydaliyyah	صيدلانيّ
medicine	dawaa'	دواء
doctor	tabiib	طبيب
dentist	tabiib 'asnaan	طبيب أسنان
pills	hubuub	حبوب
syrup	sharaab	شراب
eye drops	qatrat 'ayyn	قطرة عين
mouth rinse	ghasuul fam	غسول الفم

toothpaste	ma`juun `asnaan	معجون أسنان
bandage	<u>d</u>imaad	ضماد
liquid	saa'il	سائل

I am sick. `anaa marii<u>d</u>   أنا مريض

I do not feel well.
`ana lastu `alaa maa yuraam   أنا لست على ما يرام

It is very serious.
'innahaa <u>h</u>aalatun <u>kh</u>a<u>t</u>iirah* jiddan
إنها حالة خطيرة جداً

* <u>kh</u>a<u>t</u>iir means "dangerous" but in this context it means "serious."

I have... .	`ndii	عندي.........
stomachache	mag<u>h</u>s	مغص
headache	sudaa`	صداع
fever	<u>h</u>ummaa	حمّى
heart condition	mara<u>d</u> fil qalb	مرض في القلب
diabetes	sukkarii	سكري
blood pressure	<u>d</u>ag<u>h</u>t damm	ضغط دم
chest pain	`alam fi<u>s</u>-<u>s</u>adr	ألم في الصدر
diarrhea	`is-haal	إسهال

I feel dizzy. a<u>sh</u>`uru bi daw<u>kh</u>ah   أشعر بدوخة

Where is the pharmacy? `ayna<u>s</u> <u>s</u>aydaliyyah?   أين الصيدليّة؟

What time does the pharmacy open?

mataa taftaḥus-ṣaydaliyyah?   متى تفتح الصيدليَّة ؟

I would like something for a cold.

ʾuriidu shay'an lil bard   أريد شيئاً للبرد

I would like something for a cough.

ʾuriidu shay'an lissuʿaal   أريد شيئاً للسعال

I have a toothache. ʿindii wajaʿ ʿasnaan   عندي وجع أسنان

I have broken a tooth.

laqad kasartu sinnan   لقد كسرت سناً

I have lost a filling.

laqad faqadtul ḥashwah   لقد فقدت الحشوة

I need to go to a dentist.

ʾaḥtaaju ʾan ʾadh-habaa ʾilaa ṭabiibi ʾasnaan
أحتاج أن أذهب إلى طبيب الأسنان

Is there a doctor who speaks English?

hal yuujadu ṭabiibun yatakallamul inkliiziyyah?
هل يوجد طبيبٌ يتكلم الإنجليزية ؟

Please call a doctor.

ʾarjuu ʾan tattaṣila biṭṭabiib   أرجو أن تتصل بالطبيب

Call a doctor quickly!

ittaṣil biṭṭabiib bisurʿah!   اتصل بالطبيب بسرعة !

Have you called a doctor yet?

halit taṣalta bittabiib ba`d?   هل اتصلت بالطبيب بعد؟

Call a dentist, please.

ittaṣil bi ṭabiibil ʿasnaan min faḍlik

اتصل بطبيب الأسنان من فضلك

I want to go to a dentist.

ʿuriidu ʿan ʿadh haba ʿilaa ṭabiibi ʿasnaan

أريد أن أذهب إلى طبيب أسنان

Is there a nearby dentist here?

hal yuujadu ṭabiibu ʿasnaan qariib hunaa?

هل يوجد طبيب أسنان قريب هنا؟

Do you recommend a dentist?

hal tuuṣii bi ṭabiibi ʿasnaan?

هـل تـوصـي بـطـبـيـب أسـنـان؟

I need to go to the hospital.

ʿaḥtaaju ʿan ʿadh haba ʿilal mustashfaa

أحتاج أن أذهب إلى المستشفى

We took him/her to the hospital.

ʿakhadhnaa(hu)/(haa) ʿilal mustashfaa

أخذناه/ أخذناها إلى المستشفى

Let's go to another hospital.

fal nadh hab ʿilaa mustashfan ʿaakhar

فلنذهب إلى مستشفى آخر!

Is there a children's hospital here?

hal yuujadu mustashfaa 'atfaal? هل يوجد مستشفى أطفال؟

I am at the hospital. 'anaa bil mustashfaa أنا بالمستشفى

Is there a nearby hospital?

hal yuujadu mustashfaa qariib min hunaa?

هل يوجد مستشفى قريب؟

Take me to the hospital.

khudhnii 'ilal mustashfaa خذني إلى المستشفى

Please call an ambulance.

rajaa'an ittasil bisayyaratil 'is'aaf

رجاءً اتصل بسيارة الإسعاف

It's urgent, we need an ambulance.

'innahaa haalah taari'ah, nahtaaju 'ilaa sayyarati 'is'aaf

إنها حالة طارئة، نحتاج إلى سيارة إسعاف

Take her/him to the hospital.

khudh(haa)/(hu) `ilal-mustashfaa *(fem./masc.)*

خذ(ها)/ (ه) إلى المستشفى

She/He was hit by a car, please call an ambulance.

sadamathaa sayyaarah, ittasil bi sayyaratil 'is'aaf min fadlik

صدمتها سيارة، اتصل بسيارة الإسعاف من فضلك

What is the ambulance number?

maa raqmul sayyaratil 'is'aaf? ما رقم سيارة الإسعاف؟

Have you called an ambulance yet?
halit taṣalta bisayyaratil 'is`aaf ba`d?

هل اتصلت بسيارة الإسعاف بعد؟

Housing

house	manzil منــزل
apartment	shaqqah شقــة
to rent (v.)	yasta'jir يســتأجر
rent (n.)	'iijaar إيجــار
tenant	musta'jir مســتأجر
real estate agent	wakiil `aqaariyy وكيـل عقـاري
landlord	saahib albayyt صاحـب البـيت
deposit	albayt عربــون
lease contract	`aqd isti'jaar عقــد استئــجار
signature	taw qii` تـوقيــع
unit	wihdah sakaniyyah وحدة سـكنية
residential area	mantiqah sakaniyyah
	منطقـة سـكنية
room	ghurfah غرفــة
kitchen	matbakh مطبــخ
bathroom/toilet	hammaam حمّــام
bedroom	ghurfat nawm غرفــة نـوم
living room	ghurfat juluus غرفـة جلـوس
guest room (*see p. 109**)	ghurfat duyuuf غرفـة ضيـوف
hallway/corridor	mamarr ممــرّ

(see p. 109*)

I want to rent an apartment.

'uriidu 'an 'asta'jira <u>sh</u>aqqah   أريد أن أستأجر شقة

How much is the weekly rent?

maa huwal 'iijaar al'usbuu`iyy?

ما هو الإيجار الأسبوعي؟

How much is the monthly rent?

maa huwal 'iijaar a<u>sh</u> <u>sh</u>ahriyy?   ما هو الإيجار الشهري؟

How much is the yearly rent?

maa huwal 'iijaar assanawiyy?   ما هو الإيجار السنويّ؟

I want a three-bedroom apartment.

'uriidu <u>sh</u>aqqah bi <u>th</u>alaa<u>th</u> <u>gh</u>uraf nawm

أريد شقة بثلاث غرف نوم

Does it have a separate bath?

hal yuujadu <u>h</u>ammaam munfa<u>s</u>il?

هل يوجد حمام منفصل؟

Does the rent include the utility bills?

hal ya<u>sh</u>malul 'iijaar alfawatiir?

هل يشمل الإيجار الفواتير؟

I want an apartment with a good view.

'uriidu <u>sh</u>aqqah bi `i<u>t</u>laalah jayyidah

أريد شقة بإطلالة جيدة

I want an apartment close to the city.
'uriidu shaqqah qariibah min wasatil balad
أريـد شـقـة قـريـبـة من وسط البـلـد

In the Bar/Nightclub

bar	haanah حـانـة
nightclub	naadii layliyy نادي ليليّ
waiter	naadil نـادل
waitress	naadilah نـادِلـة
beer	biirah بـيـرة
red wine	nabiidh 'ahmar نـبـيـذ أحـمـر
white wine	nabiidh 'abyad نـبـيـذ أبـيـض
whisky with soda	wiskii bissudaa ويـسكي بالصـودا
whisky with water	wiskii bil maa' ويـسكي بالـمـاء
bottle	zujaajah/qaaruurah زجـاجـة/ قـارورة
can	'ulbah عـلـبـة
glass	ka's كـاس
dance (v.)	yarqus يـرقـص
music	muusiiqaa مـوسـيـقى
loud music	muusiiqaa saakhibah مـوسـيـقى صاخـبـة
soft music	muusiiqaa haadi'ah مـوسـيـقى هـادئـة
band	firqah muusiiqiyyah فرقة موسيقيّـة
party	haflah حـفـلـة

Let's go and get a drink.

falnadh-hab linatanaawala mashruuban

فلنذهب لتناول مشروباً

A glass of red wine, please.

ka's minan nabiidhil 'ahmar, law samaht

كأس من النبيذ الأحمر لو سمحت

Two glasses of white wine.

ka'sayn minan nabiidhil 'abyad law samaht

كأسين من النبيذ الأبيض لو سمحت

A bottle of beer, please.

qaruurat biirah law samaht   قارورة بيرة لو سمحت

The bill, please.

alfaatuurah law samaht   الفاتورة لو سمحت

Can I get you (sing., fem.) a drink?

mumkin an 'uhdir laki mashruuban?

ممكن أن أحضر لك مشروباً؟

What is your (sing., fem.) favorite drink?

maa huwa mashruubukil mufaddal?

ما هو مشروبك المفضّل؟

Would you mind dancing with me?

hal tasmahiina lii birraqs ma`aki?

هل تسمحين لي بالرقص معك؟

You (sing., fem.) are very beautiful.
anti jamiilatun jiddan أنـت جمــيــلــة جـدًا

Do you (sing., fem.) speak English?
hal tata kalla miinal inkliiziyyah? هـل تتكلمــن الإنكليزية؟

On the Telephone

call (n.)	ittiṣaal/mukaalamah
	اتصــال / مكــالــمـة
call (v.)	yattaṣil يتَّـصـل
local call	mukaalamah maḥalliyyah
	مكــالــمـة مـحـلـيّــة
domestic phone call	mukaalamah daa khiliyyah
	مكالمة داخليَّـة
international call	mukaalamah duwaliyyah
	مكــالــمـة دولـيَّــة
public telephone	haatif `umuumiyy هاتـف عمومـيّ
phonecard	biṭaaqat ittiṣaal بطـاقـة اتصـال
busy	mash-ghuul مشـغـول
extension	taḥwiilah تـحـويـلـة
hello! (phone)	alu ألـو
operator	ma'muur maqsam مأمور مقسـم

You have a phone call.
ladayyka mukaalamah haatifiyyah
لـديـك مكــالــمـة هـاتـفـيـة

Just a moment, please.

lahzah min fadlik   لـحـظـة مـن فـضـلـك

Who is calling please? man yatakallam?   مـن يـتـكـلـم؟

Is Ayman there? hal Ayman mawjuud?   هل أيمن موجود؟

No, he is away from his desk

laa, layysat `alaa maktabihi   لا ، ليس على مكتبه

He is out now. huwa bil khaarij al'aan   هو بالخارج الآن

He is on the other line

ma`ahaa mukaalamah 'ukhraa   معه مكالمة أخرى

He is in a meeting now huwa fiijtimaa` al'aan   هو باجتماع الآن

Can I take a message?

hal tawaddu an tatruka risaalah?   هـل تـودّ أن تـتـرك رسـالـة؟

Can I have him to call you?

turiidu 'an 'aqul lahu 'an yattasila bik?

تريد أن أقل له أن يتصل بك؟

Please tell him I called

qulla lahu annii ittasalt min fadlik   قل له أنّـي اتصلت من فضلك

I want to make a phone call.

'uriidu 'an 'ujriya mukaalamah haatifiyyah

أريد أن أجـري مـكـالـمـة هـاتـفـيّـة

I want to make an international phone call.
'uriidu 'an 'ujriya mukaalamah khaarijiyyah
أريد أن أجري مكـالـمـة دوليَّة

May I use your mobile phone, please?
mumkin 'an 'astakhdima haatifakan naqqaal law samaht?
ممكن أن أستخدم هاتفك النقـّـال؟

What is your telephone number?
maa raqmu haatifika?   مـا رقـم هـاتـفـك؟

My telephone number is… .
raqmu haatifii huwa… .   رقـم هـاتـفـي هـو...........

I want to send a fax.
'uriidu 'an 'ursila faaks   أريـد أن أرسـل فـاكـس

Renting a Car

car	sayyaarah	سيـارة
car rental office	maktab ta'jiir sayyaaraat	
		مكـتـب تـأجـيـر سيـارات
daily rental	ajaar yawmiyy	أجـار يـومـي
weekly rental	ajaar 'usbuu'iyy	أجـار أسبـوعـي
monthly rental	ajaar shahrii	أجـار شـهـري
I drive	aquud	أقـود
steering wheel	miqwad	مـقـود
engine	muharrik	مـحـرّك

tires (n.)	iṭaaraat	إطــارات
seatbelt	ḥizaam al'amaan	حــزام الأمــان
driver's license	rukhṣat qiyaadah	رخـصـة قـيـادة
mirror	mir'aah	مـرآة
lights	anwaar	أنـوار
seats	mqaa'id	مـقـاعـد
windows	nawaafidh	نـوافـذ
parking area	mawqif	مـوقـف
traffic light	'ishaarah ḍaw'iyyah	إشـارة ضـوئـيـة

I want to rent a car.

'uriidu 'an 'asta'jira sayyaarah   أريـد أن أسـتـأجـر سـيـارة

What is the daily rate?

maa hiyal 'ujrah alyawmiyyah?   مـا هـي الأجـرة الـيـومـيـة؟

How much do I have to pay for extra kilometers?

kam yajibu 'an 'adfa'a `anil 'amyaal al'idaafiyyah?

كـم يـجـب أن أدفـع عـن الأمـيـال الإضـافـيـة؟

Does the price include fuel?

halis si`ru yashmalul waquud?

هـل الـسـعـر يـشـمـل الـوقـود؟

I want an economical car.

'uriidu sayyaarah iqtiṣaadiyyah   أريـد سـيـارة اقـتـصـاديـة

I want a Japanese car.

'uriidu sayyaarah yaabaaniyyah   أريـد سـيـارة يـابـانـيـة

How many kilometers are included in the basic rate?

kam minal kiilu mitraat yasmalus si`rul `asaasiyy?

كم من الكيلومترات يشمل السعر الأساسيّ

I don't have a driver's license.

laa amliku ru<u>kh</u>sat qiyaadah

لا أملك رخصة قيادة

Can I use my English drivers' license?

hal yumkinunii isti<u>kh</u>daama ru<u>kh</u>satil inklii ziyyah?

هل يمكنني استخدام رخصتي الإنكليزيَّة؟

I like four-wheel drive cars.

`u<u>h</u>ibbi sayyaaraat ad-daf` ar-rubaa`iyy

أحب سيارات الدفع الرباعيّ

I don't like driving manual cars.

laa `u<u>h</u>ibbi qiyaadata as-sayyaraat <u>dh</u>aat an-naaqil al-yadawiyy

لا أحب قيادة السيارات ذات الناقل اليدوي

Age

age	`umr	عمر
child	<u>t</u>ifl	طفل
adult	baali<u>gh</u>	بالغ
elderly person	`ajuuz	عجوز
young	sa<u>gh</u>iir	صغير
old	kabiir	كبير

young man   shaab شــاب

young woman   shaabbah شــابــة

* In Arabic, saghiir صغير is the word for young and small.
  Similarly, kabiir كبير is the word for old (people) and big.
  (Old for non-human entities is qadiim قديم)

How old are you? kam `umruk? كــم عـمـرك؟

I am 31 years old.
`umrii waahid wa thalaathuun sanah
عمـري واحـد وثـلاثـون سنـة

My daughter is four years old.
`umr ibnatii arba` sanawaat عمـر ابـنـتـي أربـع سنـوات

Visiting Someone's Home

In most Arab countries, there is a special place allocated for
receiving guests. This place could occupy the whole ground
floor on one side of the building or, in apartments, a separate
room close to the entrance. The furniture in this room may
include sofas, couches, armchairs or cushions leaning against
the wall. The name of this room can vary from one country to
another:

majlis مـجـلـس (**common**)
ghurfat aljuluus غـرفـة الجـلـوس (**Gulf countries**)

ghurfat adduyuuf غـرفـة الـضـيـوف (Jordan, Syria,
  Palestine, Lebanon)
maḍaafah مـضـافـة (Bedouins) *
diiwaaniyyah ديـوانـيـة (Kuwait)

To avoid interfering with the family's daily activities, this
room is usually located as far from the living quarters as possi-
ble. Although many Arab countries no longer prohibit mixing
between men and women, you will find some other Arab countries where mixing between the two genders isn't common,
especially in the Gulf countries. So if there is a function going
on for the husband's guests, the wife, the daughters and other
female members of the family will not participate or even be
seen at the gathering. Male guests shouldn't expect to be introduced to the ladies of the house. If the guests are foreigners
and they include males and females, the females gather in the
living room and they will leave the guest room for the males.

First-time guests are treated with special care and cordiality.
They are also introduced to the rest of the guests, and then led
to the seat next to the host where the latter will engage him/her
in a polite conversation aimed at making him/her feel welcome.

If you are invited to a dinner party in some Arab countries,
you should not bring along special dishes or bottles of alcoholic
beverages as is the case in the West. You may, however, bring
some candy. If you attend a party organized for a special occa-
sion such as someone's birthday, it is polite to take along a gift.
However, don't expect that the recipient will open it right away.

When attending a gathering, you need to be careful not to disrespect any custom or belief even unwittingly. It is customary to take your shoes off before entering the guest or reception room, or even the house itself unless you see the hosts wearing their shoes inside the house.

Once seated, whether on the floor or on a chair, it is offensive to point the soles of your feet toward anyone. Pointing the soles of your shoes at anyone should be avoided no matter where you are because the sole is considered unclean and pointing it at people is considered an insult. When you are offered food or drink, try to take it with your right hand.

Expressing Thanks

Thanks	shukran شـكـرًا
Thank you	shukran lak شـكـرًا لـك
Thank you very much	shukran jaziilan شـكـرًا جـزيـلًا

Thanks to you, I have had a wonderful evening.
bifadlik kaana masaa'ii raa'i`an
بـفـضـلـك كـان مـسـائـي رائـعـاً

I appreciate your kindness. `uqaddiru lutfak أقـدر لـطـفـك

Thanks for the meal.
shukran `alal wajbah شـكـرًا عـلى الـوجـبـة

Thanks for the drinks.

shukran `alal mashruub   شكراً على المشروب

Thanks, I have had enough.

shukran laqad iktafayyt   شكراً لقد اكتفيت

Thanks for your assistance.

shukran `alal musaa`adah   شكراً على المساعدة

I am very grateful to you. mamnuunak   ممنونك

Don't mention it, you're most welcome!

laa shukr `alaa waajib!   لا شكر على واجب!

Making Apologies

I am sorry. (m) `anaa `aasif   أنا آسف

I am sorry. (f) `anaa `aasifah   أنا آسفة

I am terribly sorry.

anaa fii ghaayatil `asaf   أنا في غاية الأسف

Please forgive me. (m) `arjuuk saamihnii   أرجوك سامحني

Please forgive me. (f) `arjuuki saamihiinii   أرجوكِ سامحيني

I didn't mean it. lam a`ni dhaalik   لم أعن ذلك

I apologize. anaa a'ta<u>dh</u>ir   أنــا أعــتــذر

Please accept my apologies. (m)
'arjuu 'an taqbala i'tidhaarii   أرجو أن تقبل اعتذاري

Please accept my apologies. (f)
'arjuu 'an taqbalii i'tidhaarii   أرجو أن تقبلي اعتذاري

Saying Goodbye

Goodbye. wadaa'an   وداعـًا

Take care. diir baalak 'ala <u>h</u>aalak   دير بالك على حالك

Look after yourself. i'tani binafsik   اعــتــن بــنــفــسك

See you. 'ilal liqaa'   إلـى الــلــقــاء

Response to the above: ma'assalaamah   مـع الــســلامــة

I don't like goodbyes. laa 'u<u>h</u>ibbul wadaa'   لا أحـب الــوداع

"In Allah's protection"—an Islamic expression used to bid
farewell to someone. fii 'amaanil laah   في أمــان الــلــه

Have a safe trip! rafaqatkas salaamah   رافـقـتـك الــســلامــة!

Personal Titles

When Arabic people address one another, they do not use first names as a matter of course. Children and young people usually call one another by first names, and adults address children in the same way. The first name is quite often used within the extended family context with *yaa* يـا which is used to attract the addressee's attention:

(Oh/hey/you) Ahmad! yaa ahmad! يـا أحـمـد

After the birth of the first child, the parents may be addressed by the *kunyah* كـنـيـة. If the child's name is Hussein, for example, his father becomes 'abu husain and his mother becomes `um husain.

If a person has performed the pilgrimage to Mecca, he/she will be known henceforth by *alhaajj* الحـاج (male) or *alhaajjah* الحـاجـة (female) meaning "the pilgrim."

Respected people are called <u>*sheikh*</u> شـيـخ (male) or <u>*sheikhah*</u> شـيـخـة (female) meaning "venerable old man," "master" / "venerable old lady," "matron."

The following titles are also common:
Mr.	sayyid سـيّـد	male stranger
Madame	sayyidah سـيـدة	married lady
Miss	'aanisah آنـسـة	unmarried young woman

Brother (Omar)	'akh أخ عـمـر	more polite than calling him by first name
Sister (Amal)	'ukht amal أخـت أمـل	more polite than calling her by first name
My dear (male)	'aziizii عـزيـزي	
My dear (female)	'aziizatii عـزيـزتـي	
My beloved (male)	habiibii حـبـيـبـي	
My beloved (female)	habiibatii حـبـيـبـتـي	

Academic Titles

In the university context, a lecturer is mentioned by his academic title followed by his full name, or by his title and first name only:

(Lecturer/teacher) Ali Ramzi
al'ustaadh 'alii ramzii الأسـتـاذ عـلـي رمـزي

(Lecturer/teacher) Ali al'ustaadh 'alii الأسـتـاذ عـلـي

If a person is a Ph.D. holder, the title adduktur الـدكـتـور meaning "**Doctor**" is used:

Dr. Nader Saeed
adduktur naadir sa'iid الـدكـتـور نـادر سـعـيـد

Signs

Enter dukhuul دخـول

Exit khuruuj خـروج

Push idfa` ادفـع

Pull ishab اسـحـب

Pay Here idfa` hunaa ادفـع هـنـا

Slow Down khaffif assur`ah خـفـف السـرعـة

Caution: Speed Bump Ahead
intabih `amaamak matab انـتـبـه أمـامـك مـطـب

Do Not Enter mamnuu` adukhuul مـمـنـوع الـدخـول

Enter Only dukhuul faqat دخـول فـقـط

Exit Only khuruuj faqat خـروج فـقـط

Fasten Your Seat Belts
irbit hizaamal amaan اربـط حزام الأمـان

Keep Right haafiz `alaa masaarik al'aysar
حـافـظ عـلـى مـسـارك الأيـسـر

Left Turn Only
in`atif yasaaran faqat انـعـطـف يـسـاراً فـقـط

No Left Turn mamnuu` alin`itaaf yasaaran
مـمـنـوع الانـعـطـاف يـسـاراً

No Right Turn mamnuu` alin`itaaf yamiinan
مـمـنـوع الانـعـطـاف يـمـيـنـاً

No Parking mamnuu` attawaqquf مـمـنـوع الـتـوقـف

No Through Road
tariiq ghayr naafidhah طـريـق غـيـر نـافـذة

No U Turn mamnuu` aliltifaaf al`aksiyy
مـمـنـوع الالـتـفـاف الـعـكـسـي

One Way ittijaah waahid اتـجـاه واحـد

Road Closed attarii` mughlaqah الـطـريـق مـغـلـقـة

Wrong Way ittijaah khaati' اتـجـاه خـاطـئ

Slow! Children Playing
tamahhal `atfaal yal`abuun تـمـهـل أطـفـال يـلـعـبـون

Slow! School Ahead
tamahhal `amaamak madrasah تـمـهـل أمـامـك مـدرسة

Stop for Pedestrian Crossing
tawaqqaf li`ubuuril mushaah توقف لعبور المشاة

Parking Reserved for the Disabled
mawqif mahjuuz lilmu`aaqiin
موقف محجوز للمعاقين

No Parking at Any Time mamnuu` attawaqquf bi'ayy waqt
ممنوع التوقف بأي وقت

No Parking: Loading Zone
mamnuu` attawaqquf mantiqat tahmiil
ممنوع التوقف منطقة تحميل

No Parking This Side
mamnuu` attawaqquf alaa haadhal jaanib
ممنوع التوقف على هذا الجانب

No Truck Parking mamnuu` attawaqquf lish shaahinaat
ممنوع التوقف للشاحنات

Pedestrian Crossing
mushaah ya`buruun مشاة يعبرون

Men at Work `ummaal ya`maluun عمال يعملون

Detour tahwiilah تحويلة

Measurements

WEIGHT

gram	graam	غــرام
kilogram	kiilugraam	كـيـلـوغـرام
pound	baawnd	بــاونـد

LENGTH

millimeter	millimitr	مـيـلـلـمـتـر
centimeter	santimitr	سنـتـيـمـتـر
meter	mitr	مـتـر
kilometer	kiilumitr	كـيـلـومـتـر
inch	insh	إنـش
foot	qadam	قـدم
mile	miil	مـيـل

VOLUME

liter	litr	لـتـر
cubic meter	mitr muka``ab	مـتـر مكـعـب
milliliter	millilitr	مـيـلـيـلـتـر

TEMPERATURE

Celsius	darajah mi'awiyyah	درجــة مـئويــة
Fahrenheit	fahrinhaayt	فـهـرنـهـايـت

Major Media

Newspapers

Following is some of the newspapers published in Arabic. The English words are simply the literal meanings of the Arabic titles; they do not form part of the titles of the newspapers.

BAHRAIN
Bahrain Today   albahrain alyawm البحرين اليوم

EGYPT
The News   al'khbaar الأخـــبـــار
The Pyramids   al'ahraam الأهـــرام
The Republic   aljumhuuriyyah الـجـمـهـوريـة

JORDAN
The Constitution   addustuur الـدسـتـور
The Opinion   arra'y الـرأي

KUWAIT
Politics   assiyaasah الـسـيـاسـة
Public Opinion   arra'y al`aam الـرأي الـعـام

LEBANON
The Ambassador   assafiir السفير
Life   alhayaah الـحـيـاة
Time   azzamaan الزمـان
Daytime   annahaar الـنـهـار
Future   almustaqbal الـمـسـتـقـبـل

MOROCCO
The Morning   aṣṣabaaḥ   الـصـبـاح

PALESTINE
Jerusalem   alquds   الـقـدس
The New Life   alḥayaah aljadiidah   الـحياة الجديدة

SAUDI ARABIA
Middle East   ash-sharq al'awsat   الـشرق الأوسط
Today   alyawm   الـيـوم
The Homeland   alwaṭan   الـوطـن
The Arabian Peninsula   aljaziira   الـجـزيـرة
Riyadh   arriyaaḏ   الـريـاض

SYRIA
Baath   alba`ṯh   الـبـعـث
November   tishriin   تـشـريـن

TUNISIA
Unity   alwiḥdah   الـوحـدة
Freedom   alḥurriyyah   الـحـريـة

UAE
The Union   alittiḥaad   الإتـحـاد
The Gulf   alkhaliij   الـخـلـيـج

Satellite Channels

Aljazera Network (broadcasting from Qatar)
aljaziira الجـزيـرة

Abu Dhabi (broadcasting from Abu Dhabi-UAE)
'abu ẓabii أبــو ظـبـي

Dubai (broadcasting from Dubai-UAE)
dubayy دبـي

Al-Arabiya (broadcasting from Dubai-UAE)
al`arabiyyah الـعـربـيـة

MBC (broadcasting from Dubai-UAE)
im bii sii إم بي سي

Future TV (broadcasting from Beirut-Lebanon)
almustaqbal الـمـسـتـقـبـل

LBC (broadcasting from Beirut-Lebanon)
il bii sii إل بي سي

Arab Countries & Major Cities

ALGERIA
al-jazaa'ir   الــجــزائــر

Algiers	al-jazaa`ir	الــجــزائــر
Oran	wahraan	وهــران
Tlemcen	tilmasaan	تـلـمـسـان
Constantine	qasanṭiina	قـسـنـطـيـنـة
Annaba	`annaabah	عـنـابـة

BAHRAIN
al-baḥrayn   الــبــحــريــن

Manamah	al-manaamah	الـمـنـامـة
Almuharraq	al-muḥarraq	الـمـحـرق

COMOROS
juzur al-qumur   جــزر الــقــمــر

Moroni	murunii	مــورونــي

DJIBOUTI
jiibuutii   جــيــبــوتــي

Djibouti	jiibuutii	جــيــبــوتــي

EGYPT
miṣr مصر

Cairo	al-qaahirah	القــاهـرة
Alexandra	al-iskandariyyah	الإسكندرية
Ismaeliyya	al-isma'iiliyyah	الإسماعيلية
Aswan	aswaan	أسوان
El-Suwies	as-suwais	السويس
Dumyat	dimyaaṭ	دمياط

IRAQ
al-'iraaq العــراق

Baghdad	baghdaad	بغداد
Mousel	al-muuṣil	الموصل
Basrah	al-baṣrah	البصرة
Nassiriyyah	an-naaṣiriyyah	الناصرية
Najaf	an-najaf	النجف
Kirkuk	karkuuk	كركوك
Dhuk	duhuk	دهوك
Arbil	arbiil	أربيل

JORDAN
al-urdun الأردن

Amman	'ammaan	عمّان
Irbid	irbid	إربد
Zerka	az-zarqaa'	الزرقاء

Jerash	jara_sh_ جـرش
Karak	al-karak الـكـرك
Tafilah	a_t_-_t_afiilah الـطـفـيـلـة
Aqaba	al-`aqabah الـعـقـبـة
Ajloun	`ajluun عجـلون

KUWAIT
al-kuwayt الـكـويـت

| **Kuwait** | al-kuwayt الـكـويـت |

LEBANON
Lubnaan لبـنـان

Beirut	bayruut بـيـروت
Tripoli	_t_alaablus طـرابـلـس
Sidon	_s_aydaa صيـدا
Tyre	_s_uur صـور
Baalbeck	b`albak بـعـلـبـك

LIBYA
liibyaa لـيـبـيـا

Tripoli	_t_araablus طـرابـلـس
Banghazi	bang_h_aazii بـنـغـازي
Tubruq	_t_ubruq طـبـرق

MAURITANIA
muriitaanyaa موريتانيا

Nouakchott	nawaakshuṭ	نواكشوط
Chanqit	shanqiiṭ	شنقيط

MOROCCO
al-maghrib المغرب

Rabat	ar-rabaaṭ	الرباط
Casablanca	ad-daar al-baydaa'	الدار البيضاء
Marrakech	maraakish	مراكش
Fes	faas	فاس
Meknas	maknaas	مكناس
Aghadir	'aghaadiir	أغادير

OMAN
'umaan عُمان

Muscat	masqaṭ	مسقط
Salalah	ṣalaalah	صلالة
Sour	ṣuur	صور

PALESTINE
falasṭiin فلسطين

Jerusalem	al-quds	القـدس
Ramallah	raamallah	رام الله
Bethlehem	bait-laḥim	بيــت لـحـم
Nablus	naablis	نـابـلـس
Gaza	ghazzah	غـزّة
Hebron	al-khaliil	الـخـلـيـل
Jenin	jiniin	جـنـيـن
Toulkarem	ṭuulkarim	طـولـكـرم
Jericho	'ariiḥaa	أريـحـا

QATAR
qaṭar قطـر

| Doha | ad-dawḥah | الـدوحـة |

SAUDI ARABIA
as-su`uudiyyah الـسـعـوديـة

Riyadh	ar-riyaaḏ	الـريـاض
Mecca	makkah	مـكـة
Medina	al-madiinah	الـمـديـنـة
Jeddah	jaddah	جـدة
Dammam	ad-dammaam	الـدمـام
Abha	abhaa	أبـهـا
Tabouk	tabuuk	تـبـوك

SOMALIA
as-ṣuumaal الــصــومــال

Mogadishu	maqadiishu	مــقــديــشــو
Berbera	barbarah	بــربــرة

SUDAN
as-suudaan الــســودان

Khartoum	al-khurṭuum	الــخــرطــوم
Omdurman	um durmaan	أم درمــان
Port Sudan	bur suudaan	بــور ســودان
Kassala	kasala	كــســلا
Juba	juubaa	جــوبــا

SYRIA
suuryaa ســوريــا

Damascus	dimashq	دمــشــق
Aleppo	halab	حــلــب
Latakia	al-laadhiqiyyah	اللاذقــيــة
Homs	hims	حــمــص
Palmyra	tadmur	تدمــر
Al-Hasakeh	al-hasakih	الــحــســكــة
Tartous	ṭarṭuus	طــرطــوس
Banyas	baanyaas	بــانــيــاس

TUNISIA
tuunis تونس

Tunis	tuunis	تونس
Bizerte	binzart	بنزرت
Sfax	ṣafaaqis	صفاقس
Sousse	suusa	سوسة
Gabes	qaabis	قابس
Monastir	al-munastiir	المنستير
Kairouan	al-qayrawaan	القيروان
Jerba	jirbah	جربة
Tabarka	ṭabarqa	طبرقة

UNITED ARAB EMIRATES
al-imaaraat الإمارات

Abu Dhabi	abuu ẓabii	أبو ظبي
Dubai	dubayy	دبي
Sharja	ash-shaariqah	الشارقة
El-Ein	al-`iyn	العين
Ajman	`ajmaan	عجمان
El-Fujeirah	al-fujairah	الفجيرة
Ras El-Kheimah	ra's al-khaimah	رأس الخيمة

YEMEN
al-yaman اليـمـن

Sana'a	san`aa'	صنـعـاء
Aden	`adan	عـدن
Ta'az	ta'z	تـعـز
Al Hudaydah	al-hudaydah	الحـديـدة

Famous Landmarks

MUSLIM HOLY SITES
mawaaqi` muqaddasah islaamiyyah
مـواقـع مـقـدسـة إسلامـيـة

**Ka`aba** (Mecca – Saudi Arabia) al-ka`bah الكـعـبـة

Prophet's Mosque (Medinah – Saudi Arabia)
al-masjid an-nabawiyy المسـجـد الـنـبـوي

Dome of the Rock & Al-Aqsa Mosque (Jerusalem – Palestine)
qubbat as-sakhrah wal-masjid al-aqsaa
قبـة الـصـخـرة والمسـجـد الأقـصى

CHRISTIAN HOLY SITES
mawaaqi` muqaddasah masiihiyyah
مـواقـع مـقـدسـة مسـيـحـيـة

Church of the Nativity (Bethlehem – Palestine)
kaniisat al-mahd كنيسة المهد

Church of the Holy Sepulchre (Jerusalem – Palestine)
kaniisat al-qiyaamah كنيسة القيامة

Tourist Destinations

EGYPT
misr مصر

Cairo al-qaahirah القاهرة

Giza Pyramids ahraamaat al-jiizah أهرامات الجيزة

Mohamed Ali Mosque
jaami` muhammad alii جامع محمد علي

Al-Azhar al-azhar الأزهر

Egyptian Museum al-muthaf al-misriyy
المتحف المصري

Museum of Islamic Arts
muthaf al-funuun al-islaamiyyah
متحف الفنون الإسلامية

Coptic Museum al-mut̲h̲af al-qibt̲iyy
المـتـحـف الـقـبـطـي

Luxor al-uqṣur الأقـصـر

Temple of Luxor ma`bad al-uqṣur مـعـبـد الأقـصـر

Temple of Karnak ma`bad al-karnak مـعـبـد الـكـرنـك

Valley of the Kings waadii al-muluuk وادي الـمـلـوك

Alexandria al'iskandariyyah الإسكـنـدريـة

Almontazah Palace qasr al-muntazah قـصـر الـمـنـتـزه

IRAQ
al-`iraaq الـعـراق

Baghdad bag̲h̲daad بـغـداد

Baghdad Museum mut̲h̲af bag̲h̲daad مـتـحـف بـغـداد

Khan Murjan k̲h̲an murjaan خـان مـرجـان

Abbasid Palace qaṣr al-`abbaasiyyiin
قـصـر الـعـبـاسـيـن

Mustansiriyya School
madrasat al-mustanṣiriyyah مـدرسـة الـمـسـتـنـصـريـة

Iraqi Museum al-mut̲h̲af al-`iraaqiyy

المتحف العراقي

LEBANON

lubnaan لبنان

Baalbeck Roman City

madiinat b`albak ar-rumaaniyyah

مدينة بعلبك الرومانية

Aanjar `anjar عنجر

JORDAN

al-urdun الأردن

Jerash jara<u>sh</u> جرش

Temple of Artemis ma`bad artimiis معبد أرتيميس

Roman Baths

al-ḥammaamaat ar-rumaaniyyah

الحمامات الرومانية

Christian Cathedral

al-kaatidraa'iyyah al-masiiḥiyyah

الكاتدرائية المسيحية

Street of Columns <u>sh</u>aari` al-a`midah شارع الأعمدة

MADABA
maadabaa مـادبـا

Mosaic al-fusayfisaa' الـفـسـيـفـسـاء

PETRA
Al-batraa' الـبـتـراء

The Treasury al-khaznah الـخـزنـة

Mountain of Rum jabal ramm جـبـل رم

DAMASCUS
dimashq دمـشـق

Omayyad Mosque al-jaami` al-umawiyy الـجـامع الأمـوي

Azem Palace qasr al-`azm قـصـر الـعـظـم

Hamidiyyeh Souk suuq al-hamiidiyyah
سـوق الـحـمـيـديـة

Mount Kassioun jabal qaasyuun جـبـل قـاسـيـون

PALMYRA
tadmur تــدمــر

Temple of Bell ma`bad al-jaras مـعـبـد الـجـرس

ALEPPO
<u>h</u>alab حـلـب

Khan el Jomruk <u>kh</u>aan al-jumruk خــان الـجـمـرك

Atroush Mosque masjid al-`a<u>t</u>ruu<u>sh</u> جـامـع الـعـطـروش

School of Paradise madrasat al-jannah مـدرسـة الـجـنـة

Bab Antakia baab antaakyaa بـاب أنـطـاكـيـا

Bab El Makam baab al-maqaam بـاب الـمـقـام

HAMA
<u>h</u>amaah حـمـاة

Nawers of Hama nawaa`iir <u>h</u>amaah نـواعـيـر حـمـاة

OMAN
`umaan عـمــان

Western Hajar Mountains
jibaal al-hajar al-gharbiyy جـبــل الـحـجـر الـغـربـي

Salalah Mountains jibaal salaalah جـبــال صـلالـة

Jabal Akhdar al-jabal al-akhdar الـجـبــل الأخـضــر

YEMEN
al-yaman الـيـمــن

SANA
san`aa' صـنـعــاء

Rock House bait as-sakhrah بـيــت الـصـخــرة

The Old City Wall
jidaar al-madiinah al-qadiimah
جدار الـمـديـنـة الـقـديـمـة

Palace of Ghamdan qasr ghamadaan قـصــر غـمـدان

TUNIS
tuunis تـونـس

El Zaytuna Mosque jaami` az-zaytuunah
جـامع الـزيـتـونـة

Carthage Ruins
al-manṭiqah al-'athariyyah bi garṭaaj
المـديـنـة الأثـريـة بـقـرطـاج

Bardo Museum muthaf baardu متـحف بـاردو

Lake of Tunis buhayrat tuunis بـحـيـرة تـونـس

Kairouan madiinat al-qayrawaan مـديـنـة الـقـيـروان

Uqbah Ben Nafi Mosque
jaami` `uqbah bin naafi` جـامع عـقـبـة بـن نـافـع

El Jem Roman Amphitheatre
al-masrah ar-rumaaniyy bil-jim
الـمـسـرح الـرومـانـي بـالـجـم

Douz Oasis waahat duuz واحـة دوز

Matmata (Berber town)
manṭiqat maṭmaaṭah مـنـطـقـة مـطـمـاطـة

Hammamet al-hammaamaat الـحـمـامـات

Jerba Island jaziirat jirba جـزيـرة جـربـا

MOROCCO
al-maghrib المـغـرب

Casablanca ad-daar al-baydaa' الـدار الـبـيـضـاء

Hassan II mosque
jaami` al-hasan ath-thaanii جـامـع الـحـسـن الـثـانـي

Old Medina
al-madiinah al-qadiimah الـمـديـنـة الـقـديـمـة

City Hall saahat al-madiinah سـاحـة الـمـديـنـة

Fez faas فـاس

Gates of Fes bawwaabaat faas بـوابـات فـاس

Attarin School madrasat al-`attaariin
مـدرسـة الـعـطـاريـن

Kairaouine Mosque
jaami` al-qarawwiyyiin جـامـع الـقـرويـيـن

MARRAKECH
marraakish مـراكـش

Bahia Palace qasr baahya قـصـر بـاهـيـة

Ali Ben Youssef School

madrasat ʿalii bin yuusif مـدرسـة عـلـي بـن يـوسـف

Koutobia Mosque and Minaret

masjid wa manaarat al-quṭbiyyah

مـسـجـد ومـنـارة الـقـطـبـيـة

RABAT

ar-rabaaṭ الـربـاط

Mausoleum of Mohammad V

dariih muhammad al-khaamis

ضـريـح مـحـمـد الـخـامـس

Royal Palace of Rabat

qaṣr ar-rabaaṭ al-malakiyy قـصـر الـربـاط الـمـلـكـي

Famous Dishes

kabsah كـبـسـة

Meat or chicken served on rice

maqluubaa مـقـلـوبـة

Fried eggplant, potato, onion, tomato and nuts cooked and served on rice

mansaf مـنـسـف

Lamb seasoned in aromatic herbs and cooked in dry yoghurt "jamiid" then served on rice

msakh-khan مـسـخـن

Bread with onion, olive oil, saffron, nuts, and grilled chicken

sayyadiyya صـيـاديـة

Rice with fried or grilled fish

dulma دولـمـا

Vegetables stuffed with minced meat and rice

kusharii كـشـري

Rice, lentils, onion and spices fried and mixed together

kusksii كـسـكـسـي

Couscous, onion, meat, potato, chickpea, butter, saffron and olive oil

mahshii مـحـشـي

Eggplant, vine leaves and/or zucchini stuffed with rice and minced meat in a tomato sauce

fasuulyaa khadraa

فـاصـولـيـا خـضـرا

Lamb chops, green beans and onion cooked in tomato soup and served with rice

kibbi nayyi كـبـة نـيـة
Raw oval-shaped nuggets of minced lamb and bulgur wheat
(eaten like steak tartare)

baamyaa بـامـيـة
Okra, lamb chops, garlic and olive oil cooked in tomato soup
and served with rice

Islamic Religious Expressions

There are different Islamic formulaic terms and common
expressions that are widely used on particularoccasions. Here
is a sampling of some of the most frequent.

"**Peace be upon you**" the greeting of the Muslim
as-salaamu `alaykum السـلام عـلـيـكـم

The reply is "**And peace be upon you.**"
wa`alaykumus salaam وعـلـيـكـم السـلام

The fuller version is:
"**Peace be upon you and the blessings and mercy of Allah.**"
as-salaamu `alaykum wa rahmatul laahi wa barakaatuh
السـلام عـلـيـكـم ورحـمـة الله وبـركـاتـه

The reply is:
wa `alaykum as-salaam warahmatu allaahi wa barakaatuh
وعـلـيـكـم السـلام ورحـمـة الله وبـركـاتـه

Although this expression means "**praises belong to Allah**" or "**Thanks to God**," it is used widely as a response to "**How are you?**," as Muslims tend to thank God to express their well being.

al-hamdu lillaah الـحـمـد لـلـه

Usually said when referring to a situation in the future, e.g. "**inshaa'Allah I will go to the grocery shop tomorrow**" etc., meaning "**If Allah wills**."

inshaa'Allaah إن شـاء الـلـه

Used when someone returns from a long trip (i.e. overseas), or survives a sickness or an accident; it means "**Thanks to God for your safety**."

al-hamdulillaah `alas salaamah الـحـمـد لـلـه عـلـى الـسـلامـة

Used at the end of prayers to mean "**Please accept**."

aamiin آمـيـن

"**Allah is greater**"—also called the takbiir and used to express astonishment or excitement.

Allaahu akbar الـلـه أكـبـر

"**Allah knows best**." This expression is used to imply "I don't know."

Allaahu a`lam الـلـه أعـلـم

"**I ask forgiveness from Allah.**"

astaghrirul laah أسـتـغـفـر الـلـه

"I seek protection in Allah from the accursed Satan."
a`uudhu billaahi minash-shaytaanir rajiim

أعـوذ بـاللـه مـن الـشـيـطـان الـرجـيـم

This expression, also known as basmalah, is widely used to
begin a speech, letter, contract and/or before eating. Its meaning is **"In the name of Allah, the all Merciful the most
Compassionate."**
bismillahir rahmaanir rahiim   بـسـم الـلـه الـرحـمـن الـرحـيـم

Used after the mentioning the name of Allah meaning
"Mighty and Majestic is He."
`azza wa jall   عـز وجـلّ

"May the blessings of Allah be upon you"—used when a
Muslim wants to express his/her thanks, appreciation and
gratitude to another person.
baarakal laahu fiik   بـارك الـلـه فـيـك

"In Allah's protection"—used to bid farewell to someone.
fii amaanil laah   فـي أمـان الـلـه

"There is no power nor strength save (except) by Allah" —
used when someone is struck with calamity, or is taken over
by a situation beyond his/her control.
laa hawla walla quwwata illaa billaah

لا حـول ولا قـوة إلا بـالـلـه

Usually said upon hearing of the death of an individual, this Koranic expression means **"We are from Allah and to Him we shall return."**

innaa lillaahi wa innaa ilayhi raaji`uun

إنــا لـلــه وإنــا إلـيــه راجــعــون

"May Allah's mercy be upon him/her."

rahimahu/rahimahaa (fem.) Allaah   رحــمــه/ رحــمــهـا الـلــه

"With peace," a phrase for ending letters.

ma` as-salaamah   مــع الـسـلامــة

"What Allah wishes"—used in relation to a good omen or good tidings; e.g. if I get an A on a test, my mother might say "mashaa Allaah."

mashaa Allaah   مــا شــاء الـلــه

"May Allah bless Him and grant Him peace,"—used when mentioning Prophet Muhammad.

sallal lahu `alayhi wa sallam   صــلــى الـلــه عــلــيــه وسـلــم

Literally meaning **"old man"**—an honorific title widely used to denote scholars, as well as tribal chieftains and notables.

shaykh   شــيــخ

When a person sneezes he/she says alhamdulillaah الحمد لله ("**Praise be to Allah**"), a person who hears the sneeze says yarhamuka Allaah يــرحــمــك الــلــه, a prayer for the sneezer which means **"May Allah have mercy on you."** The sneezer then replies yahdiina wa iyyaakum Allah يهدينا وإيّاكم الله which means **"May Allah give you and us the guidance."**